DEATH OF THE BIG BOOK

A special thanks to my daughter, Karen S. Eaton. Her advice and technological assistance was vital in the book's completion.

CONTENTS

	CHAPTER	PAGE
	INTRODUCTION	iii
ONE	CATALOG HISTORY	1
TWO	SEARS CATALOG	7
THREE	THE BIG BRUISER	18
FOUR	GUNS AND TOMATOES	43
FIVE	RETAIL CATALOG	62
SIX	ED TELLING	76
SEVEN	ED BRENNAN	104
EIGHT	THE SEARS TOWER	124
NINE	REORGANIZATION	137
TEN	CATALOG RESTRUCTURE	149
ELEVEN	LEGACY LOST	165

INTRODUCTION

About 100 years after the company's birth and only nine years after its catalog division had attained a high-water mark of $3.9 billion in sales, Sears in 1993 virtually walked away from its premier catalog business. Even though Sears dwarfed its major catalog competitors, Montgomery Wards, J C Penney, and Spiegel, the company's supremacy in the catalog industry was summarily ended.

According to the Direct Marketing Association in 1992 there were 101.6 million customers that shopped catalogs by mail or phone and spent $52 billion. Even before Amazon and the explosion in the internet market, home shopping had increased 75 percent since 1983. These facts decry Sears' decision to virtually abandon its catalog business just at the dawn of internet marketing.

When Sears announced that its catalog business would close, my 33 year career ended along with thousands of catalog employees in its headquarters, four territories, six catalog merchandise distribution centers, and 2,300 selling units. The Sears catalog business had distributed annually more than 300 million forms of catalogs, 99 billion pages, and recorded 335,000 orders per day. The Spring and Fall general catalogs (The Big Book) offered 85,000 choices to customers, three times the selections of larger retail stores.

The first twenty or more years at Sears were my most optimistic and enthusiastic years in Catalog, when Sears was the nation's largest retailer and its catalog business led the industry. It was a time when many Sears' brands captured significant market share, brands like Diehard batteries, Craftsmen tools, and Kenmore appliances.

It was a golden time for employees who felt that they had stock in the company's success, were rewarded for their performance, and benefited from retirement security with profit sharing accounts and retirees' health and life insurance. Competitors envied Sears' merchandising leadership, consumer allegiance, nation-wide distribution and service network, and an enormous credit card customer base.

Even though I retired from Sears in 1993 after 33 years in Catalog, I still remain concerned for my former company's welfare just as I continue to follow my Cubbies and other favorite sports teams. It's been truly disheartening to read financial experts' reports like *Business Insider's* Hayley Peterson claim on December 4, 2016 that Sears is on the brink of catastrophe and top executives flee.

More recently, on January 5, 2017, *USA's* Nathan Barney reported that Sears Holding will shutter another 150 retail stores and sell its Craftsman tool brand to Stanley Black & Decker. The need to close stores is one matter of concern, but to sell Craftsman to a major tool competitor is quite another. Craftsman tools' brand had been a significant reason for a large segment of their customer base to shop Sears and the loss of this exclusive brand certainly doesn't bode well for the company's future.

A *Fortune* article in January 9, 2012 headlined, "How Amazon Ate Sears Lunch," an article that confirmed my belief that Sears, with its advantage of a national catalog infrastructure, should have initiated a calculated and effective transition from catalog pages to vault into leadership in the emerging world of electronic marketing.

When the Chicago Tribune reported on July 20, 2017, that Sears will sell its full line of Kenmore appliances on Amazon, it confirmed my thesis that Sears years ago had ceded its catalog business and the internet to Amazon and even today will rely on Amazon to sell its appliances as well as on its own Sears.com.

Each time I read another piece of Sears' bad news, I have taken refuge from these disappointments by returning to editing my book, *Death of the Big Book*. The book chronicles my long career with the company's catalog division that began in 1960 during Sears' 75th Diamond Jubilee Anniversary celebration and ended regrettably in 1993. My regrets haven't been lessened as Amazon's innovative actions, extraordinary growth, and aggressive plans for expansion continued to be extolled by the business media.

Death of the Big Book represents my memoir based on a thirty-three year career in the Sears' catalog division that involved interactions with many of the highest company executives and experiences that began in management of catalog stores and went on to achieve national catalog management positions.

During my career it was my good fortune to have the opportunity to have worked directly for and with a number of Sears' most talented and powerful retail and catalog executives: Edward Telling, William Bass, Henry Sunderland, Charles Moran, Edward Brennan, Jack Kelly, Charles Reaves, Everett Buckhardt, Claude Ireson, Al Stewart, and Michael Bozic.

This memoir relates my interaction with these high-powered executives through significant stages of my career that cite the actions that spurred Catalog's growth as well as highlight measures that stunted Catalog's advancement, and contributed to the company's decision to abandon its catalog business.

A popular book, *The Big Store,* authored by Donald R. Katz and published in 1987, related the intriguing power play inside the Sears Tower's executives' suites, and the efforts to develop the company's identity in the 1970s and 1980s. Mr. Katz had been given unique access and insight into the company's differences in influence and marketing strategy. Even with his admirable access to the struggles and political play on the Sears Tower's upper floors, the author overlooked the contentions that festered between the corporation's retail and catalog factions.

My final year at Sears was largely spent as a member of a task force that included several key officers and a team of Arthur Anderson consultants. Our task force was ostensibly charged to devise plans to improve the catalog company's profitability. Our work involved various revisions to Catalog's merchandising and distribution structure.

Anderson developed its recommendations to the Board from the task force's studies, and the Board concluded that almost all of the catalog structure in headquarters, distribution centers, and selling units should be eliminated.

Even though a separate catalog company was formed in 1989 under Vice President Everett Buckhardt, the Catalog's death sentence was announced in 1993. My experience led me to believe that the decision to dismantle the catalog business had been considered over time and was far from abrupt, because retail interests had eroded catalog's influence and caused the Catalog business to literally teeter for years on the corporation's shelf.

Too many corporate officials were influenced by their own retail proclivity, and viewed the catalog division as unprofitable and in competition with the company's retail stores, not a significant asset. One key company officer opined to me that he felt that the differences between retail and catalog interests could be considered a "war." Unfortunately, this incongruous view may have been shared by other retail leaders that only exemplified an attitude that led to Catalog's fate.

The displaced thousands of catalog associates, 50,000 by Chicago Tribune's account in 1993, must have been in disbelief that Sears would close the "Book" on their careers and multi billions in catalog sales, and the millions of catalog customers, particularly in the small towns, must have been confounded to learn that their years of enjoyment and ease in catalog shopping would suddenly end.

Displaced catalog personnel at every level of the Catalog organization, many with decades of service, were dedicated and motivated people that included the thousands of associates in operations and merchandise staffs in headquarters and the territories, the pickers, packers, and staffs in the nationwide network of catalog merchandise distribution centers, and the catalog personnel at counters and phone rooms in retail and catalog stores. Most Catalog Merchants and Agents, whose businesses were located in small towns throughout the country and generated about 15 percent of total catalog sales, saw their expectations of an investment and livelihood with Sears shattered.

The corporation's decision minimized the valuable synergistic benefit that retail stores enjoyed from its Catalog division. Retail stores lost the value of their customers' ability to pre-shop from the Big Books (Spring and Fall general catalogs) with their broad assortment, and even the benefit derived from catalog customers' footsteps in their stores was dismissed.

If corporate officers hadn't lost sight of the opportunity to be an Amazon before there was an Amazon, but rather emulated its past visionaries Richard Sears, Julius Rosenwald and General Robert Wood, the company might have better segued from paper catalogs to a broadened vision that exploited the immense marketing opportunities in the emerging internet. I would like to believe that Sears could mirror its founders, recapture its past success in retail, and aggressively establish its own mark in the electronic marketing revolution.

Even though In the ensuing chapters I have highlighted my perspective on some of the counterproductive measures taken that contributed to Catalog's fate and the missed potential in internet marketing, I describe the many great Sears-years that recall a rewarding career of noteworthy experiences, fond memories of dedicated associates, hosts of loyal catalog customers, a company that had a high degree of integrity and professionalism, and supportive communities that made Sears a proud and respected institution throughout America.

CHAPTER ONE
CATALOG HISTORY

Before diving into the thrust of my story, while recognizing the emergence and historic expansion in internet-marketing, it should be interesting for the readers to be familiar with some extracts from Sears Archives that chronicle the company's own remarkable growth that began as a tiny mail order business more than 130 years ago.

At a time when there were only 39 states in America, many citizens lived in rural and agricultural areas, a single general store was the prime source of supplies, merchandise had gone through a stream of wholesalers to reach the retail outlet, and many shipments came to the general store by rail.

The company's Archives describes the fateful event that provided the spark to a Sears catalog enterprise, when in 1886 a railroad agent, Richard Sears, in North Red Woods, MN received a shipment of watches from a Chicago jeweler that had been ordered by a local jeweler. When the local jeweler rejected the shipment, instead of returning the watches to the supplier, the enterprising railroad agent purchased the watches, sold them at a nice profit, and ordered more. Incredibly, that initial shipment of rejected watches inspired Richard Sears to become an entrepreneur in catalog marketing and set in motion the beginning of a giant in catalog and retail.

Motivated by his initial success Richard Sears began to sell watches and jewelry through a mail order catalog. It's interesting to note that the innovative Sears policy of "Satisfaction Guaranteed Or Your Money Back" began with an early R. W. Sears Watch Co. mailer that pronounced, "We warrant every American watch sold by us with fair usage an accurate keeper for six years – during which time, under our written guarantee we are compelled to keep it in perfect order free of charge." Such a warranty was unique at the time and later became the company's mantra.

In 1893, Richard Sears moved his enterprise to Chicago, IL where he joined Alvah Roebuck to form Sears, Roebuck and Co. In 1894 the two men published a 322 page catalog that touted, "Cheapest Supply House on Earth" and "A Book of Bargains, A

Money Saver for Everyone." In the 19th century, most farmers had bought supplies at high prices from general stores until the Sears catalog published catalog merchandise at clearly stated prices. Their first catalog featured sewing machines, buggies, bicycles, saddles, firearms, and clothing.

Roebuck sold his interest in the catalog business for the grand total of $25,000, which led to the emergence of Julius Rosenwald, a Chicago clothing manufacturer, who became an influential figure in the growth of the Sears catalog. Rosenwald became a part owner in 1895 and helped lead a growth in sales to $400,000. He later influenced the introduction of the "Big Book" with Spring and Fall catalogs in 1896, which added to the merchandise assortment with refrigerators, stoves, hand cranked washing machines, and groceries.

Catalog sales exploded from $750,000 in 1897 to $10 million by the turn of the century. To appeal to more of the American farmers' needs, Rosenwald influenced the diversification of product lines by adding dry goods, hardware, and furniture. Specialty catalogs were published, and a catalog order plant was opened on Chicago's West Side in 1906.

A shrewd businessman, Rosenwald instituted in 1907 the first expenditure cutbacks, increased advertising, promoted more adjectives in describing the merchandise features, and began the creation of a catalog empire with a network of factories that capitalized on the breadth of basic functions of design, manufacturing, distribution and merchandising.

Sears homes, that still stand today in communities all over America, were introduced in the 1908 catalog that offered an entire house kit for sale, "$725 And our free building plans will build, paint, and complete ready for occupancy this $1,000 six room cottage." The 1908 catalog also featured for $45 "Our genuine Pisani Stradavarius model violin." An electric washing machine, silk stockings, and even a motor car were offered in following years. In its history, Sears' catalogs had advertised an enormous breadth of merchandise that far exceeds the offerings of today's Big Box and Super Walmart stores.

Another major figure in Sears' history was General Robert E. Wood, a former U.S. Quartermaster General, who had joined the company in 1924. He oversaw the opening of the first Sears retail store in the Chicago catalog plant's merchandise building on February 2, 1925.

Aside from the Archives, my own Sears historical piece was contributed by my marketing professor in 1951 in a Wharton school class. He expressed his admiration of the innovative strategy that Sears employed, when in 1930 Sears began to build its retail stores in the city suburbs apart from cities' business locations. This change in retail strategy exploited the growth of the metropolitan sprawl.

This past summer, a piece of historical trivia was imparted to me by a fellow passenger on a Rhine river cruise. Frank Branca, no relation to 1940s-50s' Brooklyn Dodgers' pitcher, Ralph Branca, indicated that he read that Richard Sears had printed the Sears catalog just inches smaller than the Montgomery Wards' catalog so that the consumer would likely place the smaller Sears and Roebuck catalog on top of the Wards catalog. Frank's piece isn't mentioned in the Archives and I haven't attempted to verify its validity.

By 1931 retail sales exceeded catalog sales and registered 53.4% of the company's total sales of $180 million. This may have marked the opening salvo for retail and catalog factions' struggle for the company's attention. As the retail division gained a larger share of the company's total volume, the rivalry between retail and catalog may have been given birth.

The fact that it wasn't until 1949 before catalog sales desks were placed in retail stores could be an indication that the competition between the retail and catalog divisions had become a factor in turf protection, not dissimilar to the tug of war that I witnessed between retail and catalog factions that ultimately led to Catalog's end in 1993, when the company's retail interests overrode catalog considerations.

CHAPTER TWO
SEARS CATALOG

My career with Sears originated in 1960 in an unlikely place, a hospital room in Abington, Pennsylvania. My sister, Helen Eaton Mertwoy, a chemist at Philadelphia's Frankford Arsenal, happened to share a room with Mary Lord, personnel manager for the Sears catalog plant located on Roosevelt Blvd in northern Philadelphia.

The professional women chatted about their families. As my sister went down the list of her two brothers and two sisters she informed Mary that her 27 year old brother was being released from active duty in the U.S. Navy in June, a Wharton School graduate, married with two children, and currently serving as the U.S. Navy Controller and Supply Officer of the Harbor Defense Unit in Little Creek, VA. Mary Lord expressed her interest by suggesting that I should apply at the Sears catalog plant for a catalog sales office (CSO) management position.

In advance of my release from service, using my family's home in West Philadelphia as a job hunting base, I spent about a week engaged in interviews in the Philadelphia area that included two of the city's downtown department stores, the Container Corporation of America's plant in Manayunk, a JC Penney retail store, and the Sears catalog plant on Roosevelt Boulevard, opened by Julius Rosenwald that served as a supply base for retail as well as catalog.

In entering the huge clock tower Sears building, I was struck by the building's cleanliness and its gleaming, waxed wood floors. My sense of smell was piqued by a unique blend of aromas that emanated from the office, factory, and warehouse structure. In subsequent years, I recognized immediately the same unique smell on visits to every other catalog plant. After a meeting with Mary Lord and having completed a couple of tests, I was interviewed by the catalog sales office staff, headed by Dan J. Corry. The group impressed me as a friendly, personable, and aggressive bunch of guys, and I felt that my interview went well.

After lunch in the plant's cafeteria, we gathhered around a conference table and a staff member asked me, "George, have you ever shopped from the catalog?"

One confusing experience came immediately to mind, and I began to give my account of a shopping trip to the Sears retail store in Norfolk, VA, not far from my family's home in Little Creek, VA.

"Well, let's say I tried to shop from the catalog. I was at the catalog counter in the Sears store in Norfolk, VA, when I told the salesclerk that I wanted to buy a few things for my family and asked, 'How do I get a catalog?' The clerk said, 'I'm sorry you can't receive a catalog until you have purchased a certain amount from the catalog.' The clerk's response frustrated me and I countered, 'Huh? How can I purchase that 'certain amount' without a catalog?'"

My retort to the clerk caused my interviewers to burst into laughter and pound the table with their fists. What was so funny? I was nonplussed by their reaction, but they went on to explain that my question to the clerk was one that was repeated many thousands of times by customers like me. They went on to explain that there were just so many catalogs to be distributed, and only "a certain amount of purchases" could qualify a customer on the list to receive a catalog.

Their explanation still confounded me and it sounded a lot like Sears' version of the "Which came first, the chicken or the egg?" In stores over the ensuing years, I confronted hosts of customers that had the same question, "How do I buy from the catalog without a catalog?" I found that my own customers were similarly frustrated and they didn't understand the logic any better than I did as a customer in Norfolk, VA.

If hired, I was told that I would manage a Catalog Sales Office located in a town too small to support a retail store. The small store displayed, sold, installed, and serviced Sears brand appliances, and offered home improvement installations like fencing, water heaters, furnaces, and air conditioning. Sales clerks wrote catalog orders by phone or at the store's counter, transmitted orders by teletype to the catalog plant, received catalog customer merchandise by truck from the catalog plant, sorted and packed customer orders, stored merchandise for customer pickup, offered truck delivery of large items, or arranged for delivery directly to home by mail or truck directly from the catalog plant and factory. Customers' returns of merchandise were accepted and shipped back to the catalog plant.

A couple of weeks after a number of interviews with companies in the Philadelphia area, I received notice of acceptance from Sears, and almost concurrently the Container Corporation of America offered me a controller's position in Denver, CO.

When I discussed the two offers with my father, he encouraged me to take the Sears offer. My father, a radio technician, was a conservative and no-nonsense type of guy and a long-time customer at the Sears store in Upper Darby. Most of all, he admired the Sears Profit Sharing Plan for employees and the "Satisfaction guaranteed or your money back" pledge to customers. My father recommended that I take the offer from Sears.

At the time, Sears was touted in the industry that "Hardly anyone left Sears, because of its profit sharing program," a cherished employee benefit that had begun in 1954. Even Readers Digest touted the Sears profit sharing plan in an article that stated, "West Side elevator operators left Sears with hundreds of thousands of dollars in Sears' stock." The die was cast – I heeded my father's advice and accepted the Sears offer.

On a Saturday in June 1960, I received my release from active duty in the Harbor Defense Unit in Little Creek, VA, and I reported for training at Philadelphia's catalog plant on the following Monday morning. In the ensuing weeks, I toured every nook and cranny of a bustling plant to view packages and cartons flash by on conveyors and chutes, customers' merchandise wrapped at a furious pace in packing stations, trucks loaded to meet rigid schedules, and offices filled with busy people amid the clatter of typewriters and ringing phones.

I learned how the transmission of catalog orders from the stores were processed by the catalog plant's systems and operations: Orders were written at a catalog sales office or a retail store's catalog sales division, transmitted by teletype to the catalog plant, processed by the plant's computer, merchandise tickets were printed with destination routings, stock clerks picked small merchandise boxes and packages from rows of bins that were chuted to the computer's designated packing stations for each direct-to-customer order, or chuted to individual selling unit stations for back-to-store customers' pickup orders.

Non-mail and freight items, like curtain rods, furniture, refrigerators and fencing, were loaded onto trolleys and ticket-programmed to be pulled by chain drives to designated positions on the shipping dock. All merchandise, large and small, was shipped by truck loads to the retail and catalog stores or sent by USPS, UPS or truck direct to the customer.

Most impressive to me was the spirit of managers and workers in every position in the plant. The company's renowned employee benefits, productivity standards, contests, promotion opportunities, rewards for suggestions, and wage incentives motivated the entire plant organization of operating and merchandise managers, supervisors, system technicians, clerks, pickers, packers, and dock personnel.

In addition to Philadelphia, in my later catalog plant visits I found that same high level of enthusiasm and productivity at every level of every the plant's staff. Even when I had the unfortunate occasion to visit a catalog plant that was about to close, the dedication and pride of the plant's employees was admirable as they efficiently and conscientiously performed the closing activities.

The teamwork that was so apparent in my indoctrination tour of the catalog plant confirmed what I had studied in my Wharton Industrial Management courses that focused on the value of productivity standards and good management policy that produced good output and high morale where each individual was encouraged to do a good job and carried his or her own weight. Effective management, incentives for a job well done, affordable health and life insurance, the famed Profit Sharing program, and promise for a secure retirement instilled confidence in each and every employee that they were vested in the company's success.

At one point in my plant tour we arrived at a large glass enclosed area on one of the building's expansive floors. My guide proudly led me into an environmentally controlled computer room that housed a massive computer that was first introduced to Sears in 1957. This computer had led to the catalog plant's mechanization in order processing, merchandise handling, purchasing of goods, inventory control, and maintenance of customers' purchase records. My tour guide gushed about how their computer not only provided accurate inventory control and mechanized operations, the system also allowed for the electronic maintenance of customers' purchase records.

Prior to the computer's introduction, employees on roller skates rolled down long rows of filing cabinets to manually record every customer purchase on millions of customers' records. Computerization had eliminated the rows of cabinets that occupied thousands of square feet of floor space. The savings in payroll and floor space, and the improvement in purchase records' efficiency and accuracy contributed to a significant improvement in the catalog plant's effectiveness and profitability.

After my indoctrination in the catalog plant, I completed my training in catalog stores in the Philadelphia area. Meanwhile my family, Barbara, who was pregnant, and our two girls stayed with her parents in Bethlehem, PA. Before I was to be assigned to manage my own catalog store, I was assigned to work at the catalog's plant's first tent sale in Quaker City, PA. Fortunately,

Quaker City was only about a 30 minute drive from my family in Bethlehem.

The tent sale was a week-long event. A circus-sized tent was erected in the parking lot of the shopping center where the Quaker City's catalog store was located. Inside the huge tent, the catalog plant's surplus of children, men and women's clothing, draperies, towels, and much more were stacked high on long tables. Refrigerators, freezers, washers, and dryers, some new and some with minor dents and scratches, were lined up inside the tent and sold at sharply reduced prices. As quickly as the surplus merchandise was being sold, trucks arrived loaded with large cartons of merchandise and additional loads of major appliances.

The circus-like atmosphere was accompanied by barkers' announcements and music, and thousands of customers flocked to the event from a wide swath of the northern suburban Philadelphia, Lansdale, Bethlehem, Easton, and Allentown areas. It was a new, exciting, exhausting, fun-filled experience, even though I worked many long hours unloading trucks, moving and stacking merchandise, selling everything from T shirts to refrigerators, and ringing up hundreds of sales. Despite the long hours and fatigue all the Sears people pitched in with exemplary enthusiasm, which confirmed for me that I made the right decision to heed my father's advice and join this company.

The tent sale was designed to liquidate surplus and discontinued merchandise, and because of the sale's success the company concluded that the creation of outlets for merchandise liquidation was an effective strategy. As a result, the plant's first permanent outlet store was established in Quaker City. Where surplus and discontinued merchandise might have been disposed of through jobbers or trashed, the Quaker City outlet store's sales of surplus and discontinued merchandise contributed to a savings in merchandise losses and became a precursor to the nationwide development of Sears Catalog Outlet stores.

Soon after the tent sale, I was directed to report to Monessen, PA's catalog sales office. With Christmas only two months away, I would soon find out what a Catalog Christmas was like, and it would be a major test to my resolve to be a catalog store manager.

CHAPTER THREE
THE BIG BRUISER

Followed by my work in the midst of the flurry and fury of the tent sale, at about 2am on October 2, 1960, Barbara gave birth to our third child and our first son Gregory. Before I had the time to enjoy being the father of three and relief from the Quaker City's tent sale's windup, I was directed to report to Monessen, PA's catalog sales office to replace the current store manager, who was to be promoted to a larger catalog store.

Upon receiving the news of my assignment to Monessen, my first question was, "Where is Monessen?" I was familiar with much of Eastern Pennsylvania, because I was born and raised in Philadelphia, my best friend's family was from Scranton, PA, I vacationed with my friend's family in Wyoming, PA, my wife's family had lived in Dubois, West Hazleton, and Bethlehem, and I learned a little about a few of the other northeastern towns from my teammates on Penn's freshmen football team.

Except for Pittsburgh and the Pittsburgh Pirates, towns west of the Allegheny River were unfamiliar to me. Because I knew nothing about Monessen, I briefed myself on a few facts ahead of my trip west on the Pennsylvania Turnpike. I learned that Monessen was mainly a steel industrial town of 18,000, about 30 miles south of Pittsburgh. The town rested on the banks of the Monongahela River along with neighboring river towns of Charleroi, birthplace of singer-actress Shirley Jones, and Donora, birthplace of baseball great, Stan Musial.

After a drive of about five hours from Bethlehem, PA, my entrance into the town of Monessen and view of its Sears catalog store caused my spirit to drop like a rock. My first impression was that the town had sort of a gray feel to it. It didn't help that the small catalog store was located across the street from an enormous Pittsburgh Steel mill, which permeated the air with a hint of sulfur and ash.

Entering the store for the first time, I noted an employee busily cleaning a thin film of black grime off the gleaming white appliances displayed on the sales floor. I was informed that the steel mill's blast furnace continually belched soot that swept throughout the small town, into the catalog store, and necessitated a daily cleaning chore. Even though I would be annoyed with the daily battle against soot, I quickly came to understand that Monessen residents gladly chose the steel plant's grime and air pollution over the many lean years suffered by labor strikes and unemployment.

The Monessen catalog sales office was physically small and shallow, even by catalog store standards. To the left of the cramped sales floor's display of refrigerators, washers, dryers, water heaters and televisions, a credit department's desk was staffed by two clerks, and at the other end of the sales floor there was a counter for sales, order pickup and returns. An Allstate booth stood by the store's front counter. Behind the counter, a small manager's office was separated from a narrow cramped area with two telephone positions that received customer orders, complaints, and inquiries.

A narrow and cramped stock area was located behind a wall to the right of the counter and paralleled the street. Squeezed into the stock area were bins for customer packages, accounting and service desks, space for sorting individual customers' orders in rolling bins, and a minimal space for large item storage.

One saving grace to my first impression of the steel town and the store's space limitations was a friendly and capable staff. Everyone was experienced in their jobs in taking orders at the counter and on the phone, receiving and processing daily truck shipments of customers' orders from the catalog plant, delivering orders to customers and processing customer returns. A skilled young serviceman repaired Sears brand appliances throughout the Monessen area. Our one salesman sold appliances in the store and made outside sales on a range of home improvements, from carpeting to heating. Other associates performed credit, accounting, service, telephone sales, front desk, and shipment functions.

During the time I managed the Monessen store I recognized and appreciated the enthusiasm and dedication displayed by the entire staff. Even the Allstate agent assigned to our store's area, Walter Keck, was a valuable asset to the store. Walter recognized the importance of good customer service and would jump in at busy times to help deliver packages to customers. In the other that stores that I managed and visited over years, I was met with the same wonderful Sears spirit that represented the company exceedingly well in each community.

For a new catalog store manager, only a few months from being an officer in the U.S. Navy, there were necessary adjustments to be made from military to civilian personnel management and customer relations. The fact that the previous manager had been promoted to a larger CSO proved to be a problem. Because the previous manager had been promoted to a bigger store, I mistakenly believed that certain "conditions" I discovered since my arrival may have been deemed acceptable or overlooked by superiors - WRONG! While learning on the job and accepting things as they were, I focused on doing my best to prepare the store for my first hectic Christmas season.

Management of a CSO was not an eight hour job, more like twelve hours on good days. My tasks included overseeing and hands-on actions that included servicing customers' concerns and orders the counter and on the phone, receiving the plant's daily shipments in sorting, packing and storing packages and cartons, delivering customer orders at the counter, and receiving returns. In other words, a manager didn't just manage – he did everything.

My interactions with Monongahela valley customers were almost always enjoyable, warm, and friendly, when I was engaged in routine counter transactions and occasional selling appliances on the display floor. Most customer interchanges were just that – routine, but that wasn't always the case. Even though I had a form of retail experience in command of two of the navy's ship's stores, I found that the art of satisfying a disgruntled catalog customer, who had received a defective item or a dryer that wasn't repaired on time, was foreign to ships' stores selling cigarettes and candy to sailors under the navy's rules and regulations.

Sears guarantee of satisfaction or your money back had to be my guide, but there were times when I felt a customer's expectation was unreasonable like the return of a two year old broken toy. In coping with an angry and unreasonable customer, I learned to excuse myself, walk into the back room, take several long breaths, return to the customer, and allow the customer exactly what he or she wanted.

As a new store manager one of the things I came to realize pretty quickly was the importance of employee relations. Because my staff was mostly women, it required an adjustment from a military officer in command of men to a more sensitive and collaborative approach.

The crush of the Christmas business severely tested my ability to handle my first catalog Christmas and was almost overwhelming from long hours, chaotic activities that came too close to undoing my Sears' career before it had hardly begun.

As the Christmas season approached, it became necessary to move merchandise sorting and packing activities into the grayish basement area. The basement housed the service shop and employee restrooms. One of the basement's unpleasant features was the need to turn a valve to shut off the sewer system each night, or the basement would flood, and a foot of drainage water might greet employees in the morning.

After surviving a trying and exhausting Christmas season, in which I clocked many sixteen hour days, and only days into the New Year we were still heavily involved in processing merchandise returns and cleanup. Just as the store opened in the morning, I received a rude awakening to my Sears' career expectations, when a large, heavy-set man entered the store and introduced himself as Bob Schug, the region's auditor.

Schug was all business, and his audit proceeded to scour every aspect of my store's accounting and operations that concluded with a report listing a host of shortcomings. Though some irregularities may have been attributed to the former manager, as well as my lack of experience in an avalanche of Christmas business, the auditor made it clear to me that any attempts at excuses were unacceptable.

As soon as Schug's audit report reached headquarters at the catalog plant, Carl Shifflett, District Manager, Mildred Niekamp, Moundsville, WV's store manager, and Mabel Riffle, District Credit Manager, descended on the Monessen store and proceeded to pick me and my store apart. Mildred was a highly respected veteran store manager and was brought in to show me what it was to be a good and effective CSO manager. The slight, spectacled woman from Moundsville was a West Virginia dynamo and a whirling dervish, who swept continually through the store, exhorting the staff, "Smile, smile, everyone smile!" Mildred exemplified how a store manager should energize and relate to the store's associates and service its customers. As energetic and demanding as Mildred was, District Manager Carl's insistence on excellence in operations, and Mabel's credit activity standards were equally critical and thorough.

In addition to Bob Schug's exacting audit, operational and employee relation requirements were drummed into me by my four critics, and made me understand the high standards the company really expected of me. Instead of resentment, I respected their advice, and I tried never to forget the most important lesson I learned from that first audit - what I may think is my best effort may not be good enough. In my remaining year and a half in Monessen, I became a better manager and developed an appreciation of the importance of our little Catalog Sales Office in a small town like Monessen.

This was a period in the 1960s that preceded the invasion of large discount stores, Walmart and Kmart, into small towns like Monessen. The Sears catalog store with its catalogs that offered a large breadth of merchandise items was a distinct benefit to the community. Unlike the invasion of a Walmart, we coexisted with the local merchants. In contrast in later years, the arrival of the discount stores like Kmart and Walmart overwhelmed many small towns' local merchants and negatively impacted the Sears catalog stores as well.

In addition to my Sears duties, I participated with other business leaders in planning retail-wide sales promotions like giving away a cherry pie with every home appliance sold during the George Washington Birthday celebration and a fashion show.

During the fashion show sponsored by the Merchants Association, I took the opportunity to show off Sears' new Winnie the Pooh line of children's clothing that had become popular as a stylish, high quality and attractive children's wear. My three year old daughter, Karen, modeled the Pooh fashions and wowed the audience - I couldn't have been prouder.

In taking further advantage of the fashion event, my employees gave out catalogs in the theater's lobby, took names and phone numbers of potential customers, and later followed-up with promotional calls. I suspect that some of the fashion show's participating merchants may have been a bit chagrined at my effort to use catalogs to enlist more customers, but we continued to work together amicably on other projects.

Telephone promotional follow-up on the fashion show's catalogs led to a growth in new customers and increased sales that further convinced me in the value of telephone promotion calls as a productive sales development tool. In order to enable us to cope with a healthy increase in telephone business, I had a telephone sales room built in the basement that accommodated two telephone sales desks. I should note that the picture shown on my book's back cover was taken when I was describing to Bell telephone's rep the new telephone sales room activity with Jeanette Haddad and Margaret Cenkner.

In conjunction with a store's farm and lawn equipment sale, we created excitement and interest in Monessen by parading garden tractors down the main street. In a nearby lot, roto-tillers, lawn mowers and other pieces of garden equipment were demonstrated. Demonstrating products in action proved to be more effective than simply their appearance on the catalog page or display on the sales floor. Extra efforts like the fashion show and the farm and lawn equipment demonstrations were the type of actions that catalog stores like mine could set themselves apart from the local retail merchants.

Because the company encouraged managers of catalog sales offices to be a valuable partner in the community's retail and social activities, I became a member of the Kiwanis and sold light bulbs to finance the club's charitable work for underprivileged children. In joining the local Swedish Lutheran church, my family took great joy in the fellowship with a warm and wonderful congregation. I must admit that the congregation's delicious Swedish pastry was another reason that convinced me that our membership was a wise religion choice.

Besides the pastry I was introduced to Swedish bowling by a group of jovial church members, who guided me to their bowling alley in the church's attic. An odd, crude wooden ball was handed to me. Unlike the American ten pin ball that had two finger holes and a thumb hole, the wooden ball had a single large hole. The ball was about the size of the American bowling ball. The object of the game was to hurl the wooden ball across an alley of sawdust to knock over rows of thin wooden pins. This was significantly different from my teenage bowling experience in West Philadelphia's ten pin bowling alley on Chestnut Street. I wasn't a great ten pin bowler, but certainly better than the Swedish game. Swedish bowling was interesting and fun to play with sociable people, but too strange to play again

I left the bowling loft thinking it was my lack of Swedish heritage that made me indifferent toward Swedish bowling, but my theory was dispelled, when I later learned that my Great Great Great Grandfather, Captain John Allen was Swedish.

Monessen's mixed ethnicity of Slovaks, Poles, Italians, Germans, and Swedes was an amalgam of earnest, sociable, hard-working people. It was the community that taught me to value my relationships with the employees, customers, church congregation, business association's merchants, and Kiwanis. I even mastered the spelling and pronunciation of the more difficult Slovakian names. In fact, in my two years in Monessen, I felt I had become as fully committed and embedded in the community as if I had been born in Monessen.

Fortunately, with a great store staff, I was able to capitalize on some hard lessons and managed to steer the Monessen store in a positive direction that ultimately satisfied upper management. Growth in sales and profits and supported by a motivated staff enabled me to implement newspaper advertising, expand telephone sales payroll, and intensify promotional calls to catalog customers. Increased payroll and use of advertising was not exactly in accordance with the regional management's policy, but these marketing actions produced results and Carl Shifflett was inclined to accept my extra payroll and ad investments.

In my very first year, I had learned the value of promotional calls conducted by my telephone salespeople. I found that promotional calls conducted by skilled telephone salespersons could develop a rapport with customers, become personal sales assistants, sustain relationships over years, and thereby produce greater sales.

During key shopping periods, like Easter, Back to School, and Christmas, my two excellent telephone salespeople, Margaret and

Jeanette, contributed to the store's success in increased sales through effective promotional calling. Because Monessen's promotional calling was so successful, throughout my career I remained a staunch proponent of the promotional telephone sales activity.

In later years, retail management's opposition to the payroll investment in promotional calling and their skepticism of the value in calling a store's catalog customers to solicit sales remained an issue until payroll pressures caused promotional calling to be curtailed or abandoned in most selling units.

While in Monessen, the nation's economy had its fits and starts. Our best barometer of the economy's health was drawn from our truck driver that delivered the daily catalog plant's shipments. The number of trucks on the highway was John Sanders' measure of the business climate. John was our amiable Shields' trucking company's driver out of Pittsburgh where the Philadelphia catalog plant's shipments were staged for deliveries to the area's Sears stores.

As soon as John completed offloading merchandise from his truck and loaded returns destined to the plant, he would take the time to drink a cup of coffee and pontificate about a lot of things like, "I'll tell you, by God, when I'm on the road and I see trucks are movin', the economy's gonna be movin'." As time passed, John reported that he saw a lot of trucks on the road, "Trucks are movin' today," and sure enough Monessen's economy and our store's sales improved just as John predicted.

Paradoxically, the Monessen store's greatest competition in major appliances sales came from the Sears retail store in Uniontown, PA, about 30 miles away.

One of the more contentious points between retail and catalog factions was the conflict over appliance merchandising and pricing, because Sears own brands of major Kenmore appliances and Silvertone electronics were controlled by separate retail and catalog merchandise departments. Because of catalog and retail's merchandising and advertising disconnect, catalogs and flyers featured the same or different models on a separate merchandising schedule than retail.

33

The Uniontown retail store called me to complain about appliance prices in catalog sales flyers. But similarly I didn't appreciate the retail store's advertising of low priced loss-leader appliances. As a retail marketing strategy, the advertised "loss leaders" were designed to entice customers into the store to sell them higher priced appliances with better features. On the other hand, Catalog's merchandising approach featured a low-priced economy model, but included higher priced models with better features.

EARLY SHOPPERS DISCOUNT

Another serious bone of contention between retail and catalog arose, when the Christmas Book's Early Shoppers Discount was introduced. Customers were offered a discount on orders over a specified amount when placed by a date in October. Before the Early Shoppers Discount was established as a marketing tool, the crush of the catalog business after Thanksgiving was almost unmanageable. On the day after Thanksgiving catalog customers were like thoroughbreds at the Santa Anita track's starting gate. When the Thanksgiving bell

rang, it was as if our customers sprang out of the gate and raced to place their orders before the Christmas holiday's finish line.

The days after Thanksgiving into the early weeks of December produced a deluge of customers' orders, and the huge stream of merchandise into the stores and the catalog plants was decidedly welcome, but almost overpowering.

The Early Shoppers Discount made operational sense to the catalog business, because it advanced a significant portion of Christmas volume into October that made the order volume after Thanksgiving more manageable.

The advancement of sales made merchandising sense as well, because it alerted buyers to "runaways" (hot selling items) and offered the opportunity to increase buys on unexpected demand of particular items. Customers still bought heavily even closer to Christmas, but the Christmas sales that were advanced by the Early Shoppers discount allowed the crush after Thanksgiving to be handled more effectively.

Greater sales were enhanced even more when telephone salespeople made promotional calls and set appointments with customers to allow them time to create their discount orders, and the customers responded by building larger orders, as well as ordering even more after Thanksgiving.

Even though the Early Shoppers Discount was not only a wise operational strategy and an excellent merchandising and marketing program, retail management opposed the program. Similar to differences in appliance merchandising, retail factions believed the Early Shoppers Discount gave the company's own catalog division an unfair marketing advantage. This resentment to the discount would become just another retail-catalog dispute that would surface years later and widen the chasm further between the retail and catalog divisions.

Unfortunately, the idea that the catalog business in general was unfair competition to the retail stores was a pervasive feeling in the company and caused the discontinuance of the

Early Shoppers Discount years later despite my repeated objections.

In the two years I managed the Monessen store I had many wonderful moments interacting with customers and employees, but I had some not so great moments like the wintery day I drove through a snowstorm to seek a payment from a delinquent credit customer. Credit collection was my least favorite activity and the need to drive into a blizzard was close behind. The roads hadn't been plowed and visibility was lousy. As I entered a small mining town, my little Opel sedan was having difficulty navigating through the snow covered roads and slid off the road into a snow drift. I had purchased the German Opel in Naples, Italy while I was the supply and disbursing officer of an aviation gasoline tanker stationed in Naples. Because my Opel was without chains, it didn't handle very well on the snowbound roads, and I found it hard to believe that Germany didn't have snow like we had in western Pennsylvania. I could only imagine that Germany's Opel drivers must have had the benefit of better roads and more effective snow clearance.

Fortunately, the town's garbage truck spotted me in distress, and the workers pushed and pulled me back onto the road. But it was only minutes later and a block away that I was unable to prevent my Opel from skidding again into another snowdrift. To my horror I spied the same garbage truck down the street, and I prayed that I wouldn't be subjected to the embarrassment of the same truck seeing me in an identical predicament. Thankfully I was saved when another good Samaritan passed by and stopped to assist me in pushing and pulling the Opel out of the snow embankment before the garbage truck spotted pathetic me. Such was the wintery life of a catalog store manager at work on the snowbound hills of Western Pennsylvania.

THE BIG BRUISER

In all my years in catalog store management, the one story that stands out the most for me took place in the midst of my third Christmas in Monessen. The popular Sears Christmas Book, later renamed the Wish Book in 1968, first published in 1933, had hit America's mailboxes and sparked another huge Christmas shopping season.

It was a cold and wintery day in Monessen and only a week before Christmas. I was scurrying up, down, here, there, and everywhere. The phones were ringing off the hook, impatient customers were three deep at the front counter to place last-minute orders, pickup orders, and return merchandise – it was pure pandemonium. Merchandise shipments from the catalog plant poured in the freight door and the stock areas were bursting at the seams with boxes and packages stacked to the ceiling.

Everyone was busy trying to cope with merchandise and customers surging at both ends into the store. Jeanette and Margaret were doing their utmost to handle the flood of incoming calls, but the calls were overwhelming with all phone lines ringing or blinking on hold. Because one line wasn't being answered and rang incessantly, I had to stop running for an instant to grab the phone.

"Good morning . . . [gasp] . . . Sears!"

A woman's trembling voice stammered, "Is this the Sears store in Monessen?"

"Yes!" [Pant]

"Would you happen to have a Big Bruiser?"

The Big Bruiser was the "Hot Toy" of the 1962 Christmas season. Each year at least one toy caught fire with the imagination and desire of America's children, and this year the toy in great demand was the Big Bruiser. A TV ad portrayed a flashy white wrecking-truck, roaring off the edge of the road with its siren screaming, and its red warning light blinking to rescue victims of an accident. For many weeks, we had to advise customers that the Big Bruiser was no longer available. Every young boy in America seemed to desire a Big Bruiser for Christmas, and the demand for the Big Bruiser had cleared the shelves of retail stores, warehouses, and the catalog plants.

In spite of the madhouse that I was trying desperately to manage, there was something in the woman's quivering voice that made me pause and prevented me from responding with a quick, "No." I recalled that we had just received a single, misdirected Big Bruiser in that very day's shipment. A month or more before, when the truck was still available from the truck's supplier, another store's tele-typist must have entered our store number in error, and when the memoed (back-ordered) Big Bruiser was received by the catalog plant, the most desirable toy truck was shipped to our store instead of the ordering store.

"Yes, in fact we do have a Big Bruiser!"

"Wha'!? How in earth do you have one? Are you sure? I've called everywhere. I'm not even certain where your store is. A friend of mine just told me that there was a Sears catalog store in Monessen. Why, it's a miracle, if you have one!"

"You might say that. We just happened to receive this Big Bruiser by a mistake."

I heard a muffled sob, and the woman began to relate haltingly a heart-wrenching story.

"I live about 25 miles from Monessen . . . I have no car . . . My husband [sob] was killed in the Robena Mine explosion two weeks ago. Just a week before he was killed, he had promised our five year old son the Big Bruiser for Christmas."

Her voice trailed off into stifled sobbing. I had read of the tragic mine disaster. On December 6, 1962 at 1:06pm at the Robena Mine No. 3, 133 miners managed to escape from a dust explosion, but 37 miners perished in the mine. The woman's husband was one of the 37 that had died that day.

"Don't you worry - my serviceman will deliver the Big Bruiser to you."

The next day the Big Bruiser gift was delivered by our store's serviceman. All of us would have loved to have seen the joy of that little boy, when he spotted the Big Bruiser under the Christmas tree, but we were comforted by the satisfaction of helping one father keep a special promise to his little son on Christmas morning.

Throughout Sears there was bound to be other experiences like my Big Bruiser story that exemplified what a town like Monessen meant to a catalog store, and what the smallest Sears store meant to its community.

CHAPTER FOUR
GUNS AND TOMATOES

In the following summer, I was offered and immediately accepted a promotion to a larger store in Morgantown, WV, further down the Monongahela River and home of West Virginia University. On the day my family and I packed up to leave for Morgantown, I decided to take a few minutes to walk out to my garden to check on my tomato plants. As many of our good catalog customers would do each spring, I had purchased about two dozen tomato plants from the Sears Flower and Garden catalog.

In roto-tilling an area for my tomato plant's garden, I failed to recognize that I was about to plant my garden smack dab in a field of poison ivy. I only realized what I had done, when a fierce, itchy rash spread over my face, arms, and legs. Over the ensuing months the poison ivy rash disappeared, but I had stayed clear of my tomato garden for fear that the surrounding poison ivy would deliver another deadly dose.

Since we were moving, I thought I should at least take one last look at my tomato plants. It was an awesome sight. For months without cultivating, fertilizing, or watering, I discovered that my little plants, grown in a field of poison ivy, had blossomed into lush rows of beautiful, large tomato plants and were burdened with a bountiful crop of tomatoes that would have made any tomato farmer proud.

During my college years I had worked in a cousin's plastic factory that manufactured pen sets and show cases for the Esterbrook pen company. In the summer months, I made a few trips to the Esterbrook's Camden, NJ offices. Since the Campbell Soup plant was near the Esterbrook facility, I was impressed at the sight of a long line of large open trailers loaded to the brim with Jersey grown tomatoes destined for Campbell's soup kitchen. My tomato crop wouldn't have made a truckload – maybe a pickup, but it certainly wouldn't qualify for the Campbell Soup Company. On the drive to Morgantown, I regretted that poison ivy caused me to leave baskets of quality tomatoes behind.

To this day after numerous attempts and loving care, I've never been able to even come close to my first and only success in growing tomatoes. Too much care, too little care, too much water, too little water, too many birds, and too many bugs led to a succession of tomato gardening failures. Even in retirement, with plenty of time to perfect a tomato gardening technique, I've since been forced to surrender to Mother Nature and resigned myself to the fact that I was destined to never master again the intricate art of tomato farming.

The Morgantown CSO had the same cooperative, dedicated, and efficient staff as Monessen and almost all of the catalog units I managed or visited in future years. Even the store's customers in Morgantown were no different than the customers I left behind in Monessen, but other factors made the move to the Morgantown store like a dream come true. The battle with the soot belched from the steel mill's furnace was over. West Virginia University's home contributed to a nice, clean, college-town feel. The store had greater sales volume, sufficient floor display area, ample storage space, and a separate four position telephone sales room.

Luckily, we were fortunate to find a beautiful and affordable home to rent from the state's education superintendent, who had moved to the state capitol in Charleston. The commute to the store amounted to a three minute walk. My new home was across the street from Morgantown's high school and a little bit more than the length of the school's football field to the catalog store's back door.

On my first day in the Morgantown store I sat down with Ken, the store's lone salesman, who confided to me that the previous store manager had a habit of interfering in appliances sales that should have been credited to him. When Ken informed me of the former manager's invasive practice, I imagined my predecessor resented his salesman's greater earnings, or he thought he was controlling payroll by avoiding Ken's commission. At that time, it wasn't unusual for a salesman's commission to exceed a catalog store manager's minimal salary. But whatever his motivation, I concluded it was the previous manager's short-sighted thinking to limit the salesman's initiative and compensation. It was a bad practice and wasn't beneficial to the store's performance.

My response to my salesman: "Ken I want you to sell! Your success means the store's success and my success - SELL!" Happily, Ken proved he could sell and did sell extremely well. Ken was supported by the entire staff by developing leads (prospective customers) for the salesman's follow-up.

Only a week or so after my arrival I discovered that the credit department needed help. The store's credit manager asked me to accompany her on a repossession of a shotgun and a bicycle. Even though any repossession activity was distasteful for me, I agreed to accompany my credit manager to the delinquent customer's home - a decision that I would soon regret.

We drove a good distance out of town on a country road until my credit manager turned off onto a bumpy and rutted dirt road that skirted past the rears of sad, ramshackle, unpainted homes. Vintage laundry equipment stood on back porches, gray clothes hung on backyard lines and over houses' railings, an array of rusted and unrecognizable junk was scattered in back yards, and inoperable rusted, beat-up cars and trucks were strewn about. Immediately the thought came to my mind that that our delinquent customer living in such an impoverished area didn't promise success for our credit collection.

Finally, we came to a stop at our customer's rutted, dirt driveway that was too steep for the car to safely drive up to the house. Forced to walk up the driveway, we plodded upward to finally reach sight of our customer's house and its surroundings. It was hard to say which was more distressing, the house's dilapidated condition or the dreary and cluttered surroundings. It was obvious to me that we shouldn't have sold anything on credit to these people. Onto the porch that lacked a few floorboards, we stepped gingerly up to the front door. The credit manager knocked a couple of times on the door. We waited several minutes, but no sound came from within. I knocked harder on the door. My knock was met with muffled voices coming from upstairs, and a few moments later a little, stark naked boy opened the door.

"Where's your parents son?"

"They're yuckin' upstairs."

Taken aback by the little boy's announcement and too embarrassed to look at my female credit manager's reaction, I suppressed a cough and said, "Please tell your parents that folks from Sears are here."

The boy disappeared and after ten minutes or so, a tall, bony, barefoot, bearded man, dressed only in overalls, appeared at the door.

"Good afternoon, I'm George Eaton, manager of the Morgantown Sears store. I'm here with our store's credit manager. Our records show that you've not made any payments on your account, and we're here to receive full payment on the amount due from your purchase of a shotgun and a bicycle."

"[Yawn] So?"

"Unfortunately, if you're not prepared to make the necessary payment, I'm afraid we're going to have to take the gun and bicycle with us"

The man scowled, snorted and uttered a few unintelligible words under his breath, and he then turned slightly away to reach for something inside the doorway. The something became a most unfriendly looking shotgun, and the holder, with his bony finger on the trigger, lifted the gun's barrel toward my chest and spoke in a slow, deliberate, country drawl.

"Wahl . . . mister . . . this hyar's the shotgun . . . and . . ." He waved the gun's barrel inches from my chest and then swung the gun's aim out to the yard to point at a twisted piece of metal in the barren, trash strewn, front yard. "Thar's the bicycle and yew can tek . . . the damn bike, but yew besn't . . . tek my gun."

The shotgun still looked plenty operational, but the twisted, rusted thing in the yard bore little resemblance to a bicycle. The man's unpleasant demeanor and armed threat caused me to blurt, "NO SIR! You can keep the gun and the bike!"

The gun-toting man's threat motivated me to spin and retreat from the scene. I had no intention in "taking a bullet" for Sears and might have recalled my mother's past admonition, "Geordie, discretion is the better part of valor." Without looking back I put discretion into motion and headed for the driveway.as fast as my legs would allow. My credit manager managed to follow close behind on my heels as we hastened back down the dirt driveway.

On our somber drive back to the store, I informed my silent driver, "A person like that should never have been extended credit.

Please don't count on me to go on another repossession trip and please don't ever give me reason to do so."

Thankfully that was my very last repossession action.

Not long after that horrific experience in the backwoods of West Virginia, a new credit staff, Alice and Beverly, took over and did a terrific job in straightening out the department by putting all accounts in proper shape and making further repossessions unnecessary.

My strange encounters in Morgantown didn't end there. One lazy summer afternoon, while I was manning the front counter during my staff's lunch-break, a tall man burst through the front door. He flew past the appliances in the store's showroom, and stomped toward me with a rifle in hand and a fierce look in his eyes. When he reached the counter, I was shocked to see that one side of the man's face had been burned a bright blue with brilliant streaks of crimson. My eyes were next drawn to the gun's condition that didn't look much better than the man's face.

"THIS GODDAMN ENFIELD RIFLE BLEW UP IN MY FACE!"

Threats of a million dollar suit immediately came to mind, and I stuttered, "That's awful! Wha' . . . wha' . . . can I do for you sir?"

"*DO*?! YOU CAN TAKE THIS DANGED GUN BACK AND GIT ME ANOTHER ENFIELD!"

"YES SIR!" I exclaimed while heaving an enormous sigh of relief. Before the man might seek a lawyer, I must have broken a record in the time it took me to complete a return document and write a reorder a new Enfield rifle for the injured customer. As soon as the Enfield's victim seemed satisfied and turned to walk away, I breathed another sigh of relief, but was disturbed by the fact that within only a few months in Morgantown this was the *second time* I've had a gun pointed at me.

As months passed in Morgantown, my newly motivated salesman proved to be an excellent appliance and home improvement salesperson. With the help of an energized staff, Ken sold appliances and home improvement fencing and furnace jobs at a record pace. The salesman was aided by leads/referrals from every employee in the store, on the phone, at the counter, and from the credit department. It was a team effort.

Morale began to soar as hard work produced wins in regional sales contests that enabled us to afford a couple of store-wide parties with prize monies issued from the regional office. Our store took pride in selling more Sears bio-degradable laundry detergent than any other store in the region. Use of suggestion selling on every customer contact led to hardly a person in Morgantown and the surrounding hills and valleys that didn't know of or hadn't bought a box of Sears Bio-degradable Laundry Detergent. The detergent's bio-degradable feature was a significant selling point for many customers with wells and septic fields.

Our little store had a distinct advantage over the local merchants, because of catalog's wide range of merchandise and services. Also we had the benefit of national and regional catalog headquarters sales promotions, signage, and contests that were designed to guide and energize the selling units.

Morgantown's teamwork nurtured job satisfaction and provided a focus on the store's success. After only one year, the store's success led to my promotion to a larger and higher sales volume store in Atlantic City, NJ.

When regional headquarters proposed the Atlantic City manager's position to me, I had accepted without hesitation. Carl, concerned that I would be leaving his district, questioned me, "I thought you were happy in Morgantown. Why did you so readily accept the Atlantic City store position?" I explained to Carl that I loved Morgantown, but with my wife being pregnant and three young children I was stressed from living paycheck to paycheck. I felt that the only route I could take, or any catalog store manager could take for that matter, was to move to the next larger store with its higher salary.

Before my transfer to Atlantic City I attended an enthusiastic meeting of all of the region's catalog store managers. It was as close to a collegiate pep rally as any promotional meeting could hope for. Key catalog merchandise managers from headquarters were introduced and one particular prestigious merchant was serenaded by an enthusiastic crowd to the popular song, *Hello Dolly,* replacing "Dolly" with the celebrated merchant's name. Merchandise offerings were presented with great humor, enthusiasm and professionalism. It was the rousing kind of meeting that was designed to motivate managers like me, and it exemplified my earliest memories of the Sears catalog spirit.

As fate would have it, the Morgantown Merchants Association had selected me to chair the town's next annual retail promotion. It may have been an honor to chair the town's big sale event, but I actually felt relieved that with my promotion to Atlantic City I had escaped the demands of directing the town's retail event.

The Atlantic City store was a unique building, because it had been a theater at one time and conversion to a catalog store's layout allowed for an unusually large floor space for merchandise display, unlike limited display space in many other catalog stores. The Atlantic City CSO was greater in sales volume and space and included a large service department that serviced the entire South Jersey's coastline. In 1963, the store was located on the city's main street, Atlantic Avenue, in the center of a still thriving, pre-casino, family-friendly vacation destination, and just a few blocks from the beach and the famous entertainment center, *Steel Pier*.

Shortly after my family moved into our home in nearby Somers Point, NJ, our fourth child and our second son, Scott, was born in the Somers Point hospital.

Within one year in Atlantic City, the store's appliance and home improvement sales began to grow, when I increased the salesmen staff from one to four. Led by an effective and aggressive service manager, the service department made a significant contribution to the store's success. The service technicians and clerical staff were encouraged to increase service calls' productivity and maintenance agreements (extended warranty) sales that resulted in the department's recognition for its profitability improvement. Guided by their training, when a serviceman discovered an appliance that would be uneconomical to repair, a lead for a salesmen's follow-up was generated - a text-book case of synergistic teamwork.

Benefiting from experiences in Monessen and Morgantown, I had learned how much motivation and internal promotions could enhance teamwork, morale, and enthusiasm in a store's staff. Atlantic City's employees responded enthusiastically to fun, in-store promotions where the sales and service staffs were divided into competing teams, Atlantic City Mets versus the Brigantine Beachcombers.

When the Mets salespeople made a significant sale or a Mets serviceman sold a maintenance agreement, a large ship's bell was rung. If the Brigantine Beachcombers' team made a big sale, an air can's fog horn was blared. This fun-filled approach to an in-house contest resulted in increased merchandise sales and maintenance agreements and represented the type of promotions that I and other store managers employed to motivate and excite their staffs to attain their stores' goals.

There seemed to be at least one experience in each one of the stores I managed that were most memorable, and that "one" in Atlantic City occurred on an especially hot summer day. With the benefit of a large sales floor, we were in the midst of a big in-store sale, at least big for a catalog sales office. All categories of the plant's surplus merchandise with sharply reduced prices had been delivered to our store. Draperies, towels, clothing items, etc. were stacked on long tables, and the store was hopping with shoppers.

Our single cash register was humming. The four salesmen were busy demonstrating a large selection of washers, dryers, freezers, and refrigerators that had been shipped from the catalog plant specifically for the sale. The appliances featured big discounts on discontinued and slightly damaged models. It was a very small version of my experience with the Quaker City tent sale.

While all this activity was going on, I was busy conducting an electric carving knife demonstration at the store's front window, carving slices from a large baked ham. A number of shoppers in the store as well as a small crowd of locals and tourists gathered outside the store were witnessing my carving demonstration. I attempted to impress my audience by carving extra thin slices of ham. In the midst of my demonstration, a salesclerk rushed up and informed me that the district manager, Harry Beideman and the new regional catalog sales office manager, Dick Lamb, had just arrived through the store's back door. Immediately, I ceased the demonstration, disconnected the knife from its cord, and went back to greet my two visitors.

After introductions, I escorted Lamb and Beideman out onto the sales floor, and they seemed to be impressed by the event and all the surrounding activity. By the time we returned to my carving knife demo location at the store's front, I quickly recognized that the electric carving knife had disappeared from the table, but the knife's cord and ham were still there.

I immediately shouted, "DAMN! Someone walked off with the carving knife, but the *dumb bastard* didn't take the cord!"

A small, squeaky voice behind me asked, "Won't it operate without the cord?"

When I turned to locate the questioner, I came face to face with a short, round, bearded man, cloaked in a heavy, woolen overcoat. My questioner was an unusual sight to behold, because it was 95 degrees outside, and the man wore a heavy and frayed winter coat that would have been better suited for the coldest wintery day in Chicago. Instantly, I surmised that this was the "dumb bastard" that had stolen the knife, but all I could do was state in a disgusted voice, "NOOOO, it won't *work* without the *cord*!"

At that, I glared at my suspected and disappointed thief, who slowly turned, waddled away, and exited the store. There was no doubt that the man left the store with the inoperative electric carving knife stashed somewhere in the recesses of his ratty winter coat.

This being my first encounter with Dick Lamb, I was pleased that he complimented me on my sales event, but later disappointed by his dissatisfaction that my salesmen's prospect file wasn't up to date. Every lead/prospect a salesman received, a copy was kept in the manager's prospect file to monitor the salesman's follow-up on customers interested in an appliance or home improvement. It may have been a minor detail in light of the day's event, but it was just another experience that even when you may think you have given your best effort it may not have been good enough.

Before my year at Atlantic City had elapsed and still barely living from paycheck to paycheck, I submitted a request to transfer to the retail side of Sears, because I felt I had proven I could manage the largest catalog store, and I believed that retail management might offer me a greater opportunity in advancement and improved income than my remaining within the catalog store organization.

When I applied for a transfer to retail, Dick Lamb and catalog's regional office didn't object to my transfer, and I was invited to an interview with the territory's personnel department.

Soon after my interview with Eastern Territory's personnel management and after only one year in Morgantown and Atlantic City, I learned that my request for a transfer to retail was accepted by Dick Lamb and the CSO organization. Lamb and I were destined to cross paths again in a much more significant way.

CHAPTER FIVE
RETAIL CATALOG

My transfer to retail was confirmed when I was directed to report to Bill Bates, store manager of the new Sears Landmark store in Alexandria, VA. My new assignment would be the Landmark store's satellite manager. The satellite unit replaced the former catalog sales office, which was located only a few miles down Duke Street from the recently opened retail store.

The move to Alexandria proved to be fortuitous, because Bill Bates had been the Boston catalog plant's regional manager, and he became a most supportive mentor in my introduction to the retail organization. Not only was Bates an excellent A store (a full merchandise lines retail store) manager, his previous position in Boston equipped him with an understanding and appreciation of the catalog business, and he supported everything that I tried to do to expand the satellite's sales.

As soon as I arrived in the Alexandria satellite, the former catalog sales office was renamed a Catalog Sales and Appliance

Store. Even though management of the satellite was no different than managing a CSO, I was introduced to the retail organization and the segment of the catalog business, known as Division 200.

As disappointed as I had been in the space restrictions of the Monessen catalog sales office the Alexandria satellite's facility was equally challenging. The sales floor's size was a fraction of the Atlantic City store's sales floor. In fact the entire store was even smaller than the under-sized Monessen store. At Bill Bates' direction, the retail store's display staff did a terrific job in improving the display of appliances and televisions in the minimal available floor space.

During the Christmas season, the store's backroom space was so meager; shipments had to be processed apart from the store in a garage a block away. An eight position telephone unit was isolated on the second floor of an office building directly across Duke Street. At first, the telephone unit's size appeared to be the only saving grace to my transfer to retail. As a CSO the Alexandria store had a highly successful telephone business. With the opening of the retail store and its own catalog division, the satellite's catalog business was sharply reduced, but Bates insisted that I continue to staff all eight telephone positions. It was unusual for most management to endorse greater telephone sales payroll, but it was indicative of the level of the retail manager's support that I enjoyed.

My working relationship with the retail store's staff couldn't have been better, including the store's controller, Bill Spicer, who could be as amusing as he was expert in his job. Spicer and I crossed swords on only one point – his determination of the satellite's profitability.

The satellite's expenses were buried in the official retail store's profit and loss Statement (P&L). In order to determine the satellite's profit performance, an unofficial P&L was created by Spicer. In addition to the satellite's expenses that could be isolated, the controller would allocate a portion of the retail store's administration costs onto the satellite's informal and engineered profit and loss statement. My objections to Spicer's allocations of the retail store's expenses onto the satellite's monthly P&L led to a number of intense, but amiable encounters with the controller.

THE ENGINEERED PROFIT AND LOSS STATEMENT

Bill Spicer's engineered Profit and Loss (P&L) statement for the Alexandria satellite was my first introduction to a document that frustrated me and had a much greater implication further on in my career. I would later learn that an annually produced National Division 200 P&L statement would contribute to top management's wrongful perception of the Division 200 business' profitability as well as the total catalog business' contribution to Sears.

Because the company's retail catalog activities, designated Division 200, wasn't a stand-alone business in retail stores and satellites, company officers relied on the annual engineered study prepared by the national operations staff. The complex study measured profitability from revenue and all costs attributed to retail-catalog units to produce an Annual National Division 200 Engineered Profit and Loss Statement.

Unfortunately, each year the company's nationally engineered Division 200 P&L, that represented about one-half of total catalog sales, contributed to the impression that retail

stores' catalog business was unprofitable and the total catalog business was unprofitable or marginally profitable.

Aside from the skepticism of catalog's profitability, too little regard was given to catalog's synergistic value to the retail stores, even though company's studies repeatedly concluded that customers with catalogs benefited retail stores' sales by pre-shopping from catalogs at home, as well as adding catalog customers footsteps in the retail stores.

In the midst of one of my monthly P&L sessions with the controller, I once again objected to Spicer's allocation of certain expenses onto my unit's P&L. Instead of trying to justify his calculations or even recognize my objections, Spicer peered up from the P&L document, smiled and exclaimed, "Damn Eaton! You're wearing so many freakin' medals you look like a goddamn Mexican general!!"

Spicer was so amused at his remark that he almost fell back out of his chair while roaring with laughter. As he would often do, the controller not only ignored my complaints, he took this occasion to ridicule the several pins I wore on my jacket and tie: A Sears five year pin, a Civitan club pin and a Craftsman tie-tack. His attempt at humor at my expense was pure Bill Spicer, but the humorous and friendly controller still didn't give me a break on the expense allocations.

In visits to the Landmark store I did my best to help Paul, the youthful store's Division 200 manager. Paul was intelligent, aggressive, impulsive, and personable, but he had a lot to learn in running a major store's catalog department. When I or other store management tried to explain a procedure to Paul, he would smile, stand erect, click his heels together, and respond, "Yes sir!" You had to like the guy.

One memorable day, only a few days away before Christmas, I visited the retail store and passed by the catalog counter where I was shocked to see a large crowd of mumbling and grumbling catalog customers. A counter sign indicated that the next customer to be served was number 28. With the thirty or more irritated, impatient, and shuffling customers waiting to pick up their Christmas orders or return merchandise, it was obvious to me that there wasn't nearly enough staff at the counter to handle that horde.

Without hesitation, I rushed into the stockroom to discover the young catalog manager seated at his desk.

"Jesus! Paul, you've got a mob out there! You've got to get some help out there!"

The young man leaped out of his chair, clicked his heels and declared, "Don't worry George, I'll handle it!"

Sadly, he wasn't about to handle it too well. I followed Paul out to the counter, but I couldn't remain to help him – I had my own Christmas crowd to take care of back down Duke Street.

I lingered just long enough to hear Paul shout, "RETURNS OVER HERE! YOU DON'T NEED A NUMBER!!"

That was a *huge mistake* to announce to a grumbling crowd, whose patience had already run thin. Most had waited a considerable amount of time only to be told that their number in line was being ignored. Paul's declaration caused an eruption of an angry roar that must have shaken the popcorn maker a floor below and reverberated throughout the store. Unwittingly, Paul had thrown gasoline on the proverbial fire, and he could have faced the first ever lynching in a Sears store. They were seriously angry people, and there was no way of saving Paul, so I retreated to the store's exit as fast as I could. I couldn't stand the sight of blood.

The young manager survived his first Christmas and still required more catalog management experience, but I later discovered that Paul was a darned good carpenter. Because I had concocted a system that I thought might help inexperienced people like Paul, I enlisted Paul to help me build my first "Six-a-matic." Because I was dangerous with a tool in my hands, and still am, Paul agreed to build the "Six-a-Matic" with the display department's scrap wood. I had conceived of a simplified filing and order follow-up system that would help maintain a uniform follow-up on incomplete customer order shipments.

I could have called the system anything, but "A-Matic" was a popular term and the six file compartments fostered the "Six-a-Matic" name. Five of the slots represented the week's five shipment days and the sixth slot was for special orders, factory, and mail-in orders. Above each slot were instructions on follow-up procedures on the previous days' shipments. For example, if a shelf item (small-package) from the previous day's shipment failed to appear in today's shipment, the instructions above the slot were to cancel the item out and reorder the missing item. Car items (larger packages) not received as of the third day would be cancelled and reordered. Large freight items, based on their characteristics and schedule, were similarly culled. In this way incomplete orders were culled and missing items reordered on a consistent schedule. In practice, the system worked well.

A few years later, the Six-a-Matic concept was accepted by none other than Carl Shifflett, my former district manager, who had been promoted to a national operations position in headquarters. Carl directed the manufacture of my invention in sheet metal and produced the Six-a-matic for national distribution. My former boss had built a national reputation as an excellent administrator and operator, two attributes that had impressed me as his store manager in Monessen and Morgantown.

As manager of the Alexandria satellite I followed the company's lead in community service by joining Alexandria's Civitan Club. The Civitans' mission was to benefit the mentally handicapped and an annual sale of Claxton fruitcake financed their efforts. The

Alexandria's Civitans were an aggressive, socially-conscious bunch, and I became deeply involved as co-chairman in their plan to develop Camp Tapawingo, a camp for mentally handicapped children. The club owned a wooded tract near Manassas, VA that had been used by the Boy Scouts. Camp Tapawingo's objective was to provide a real camping experience, under tents, for mentally handicapped children.

Volunteers' work began with the equipping of the existing mess hall's kitchen with donated restaurant-grade appliances and one Saturday afternoon was spent painting the large wooden building with creosote. Sites for tent platforms were located and built around the wooded property, and a large septic field was excavated. It was a major project that required a lot of planning, fund raising, and hard work. A host of volunteers from the Civitan Club and members of associations for mentally handicapped children joined together to make the camp a reality.

By my second year in Alexandria, managing the satellite had become routine, which allowed me to spend many hours in Camp Tapawingo's planning and overseeing of the camp's construction.

The camp opened on July 9, 1966 with 80 campers and a supporting volunteer staff of 45.

On opening day, I was dressed in a T shirt and shorts, and as I passed by a circle of campers and their counselor, I heard one of the young campers ask his counselor, "Is that one of the new boys?" Being identified as one of the youthful campers tickled me, and made me think that I must have done a better than average job in associating myself with the program. The camp's first summer was successful and extremely satisfying to me and everyone involved in its development.

In my second Christmas season in Alexandria, as busy as it was, I committed myself to chair the Civitan's annual fruitcake fundraising drive. Unlike most fruitcake gifts that never get eaten, but are "re-gifted" from one year to the other, I found Claxton fruitcake to be pretty tasty as fruitcake goes. Even if our buyers didn't enjoy fruitcake, they could take satisfaction in the fact that their purchase supported programs like our Camp Tapawingo.

It was a week into 1967, when I learned that Bill Bates wanted to meet with me and Bob Hannigan, the Washington Group D/200

Manager. Bob and I had a good working arrangement. I believe he may have initially taken notice of me, when I attended my first D/200 managers meeting at the DC distribution center. One of the managers commented, "With all of the Washington Group's catalog managers in this same room, what would happen to catalog in the Washington Group's area if a bomb went off in here?" I smiled sarcastically, "It would probably take them about one hour to replace us all." My quip was received by the group as a joke and got a big laugh in the room, but I wasn't kidding.

The meeting with Bates began with a shocker, when he suggested that I assume management of the retail store's catalog department as well as the satellite. He went on to propose closing the satellite's telephone unit and combining its staff with the retail store's telephone unit that had ample desks to accommodate all of the satellite's telephone salespeople.

"What do you think?" The store manager leaned well back in his chair and waited for my response.

I glanced at Bob Hannigan and saw from his frown that he wasn't happy with Bates' surprising proposal. When Bob attempted to offer his opinion, Bates waved him off and turned again to me for an answer. My mind then accelerated into high gear to weigh the store manager's proposal: My wife and our four children deserved more, I felt unchallenged for a long time, the proximity of the two stores had made competition between the two telephone units impractical, and my new dual position might be the ticket for further advancement in Sears.

When the dust had settled at the conclusion of my second Christmas season, Bill Bates must have concluded that I was capable of doing more than managing the satellite. He must have taken note that I had managed my store through the hectic Christmas season as well as directed the Civitan's fund raising.

With a quick calculation of the pros and little cons, I said, "I can do it. It makes sense."

Bates beamed in approval, but Hannigan's jaw dropped in disbelief, because he knew how hard I had competed with the retail store's Division 200. Even though I was convinced that the satellite needed its own telephone sales unit for the small store to flourish, I knew too well that the proximity of the retail and satellite stores made the two telephone units uneconomical and counter-productive.

As fate would have it, I would confront the question of each selling unit having its own telephone sales force as a major issue again at much higher levels in the company's discourse.

In the following several months, the combined telephone units and increased attention to the retail store's D/200 unit proved to be a good move with a significant increase in overall units' catalog sales. Even though the combined performance of the two catalog units was successful, order pickup and store traffic in the satellite fell off and the satellite's appliance sales began to suffer. Because the satellite no longer had its own telephone sales unit to promote its own store exclusively for order pickup and major appliance sales, the move to combine the telephone units in the retail store delivered a significant blow to the satellite store's sales.

Bates' decision and my support proved to be the right move for Sears in the Alexandria market, and it wasn't long before I would discover that my agreement with Bates was destined to be beneficial for my career in a most fortuitous way.

CHAPTER SIX
ED TELLING

In the following summer, I had become comfortable in managing the satellite and the retail store's Division 200. I was slated to be the Alexandria Civitan club's President, because the Civitan's fruitcake chairman was traditionally elevated to president in the ensuing year. But once again I was destined to avoid another community task, when Bill Bates informed me that I was to report for an interview with Ed Telling, retail stores' New York Group Manager.

The New York Group was one of the corporation's largest and a most important retail market, and Ed Telling was purported to be a rising star at Sears. The New York Group of retail stores encompassed New York City's five boroughs, extended east on Long Island, south to Watchung, NJ, north to Stamford, CT, and west to Morristown, NJ.

At the time of my Telling interview in 1967 the New York Group offices were located temporarily on the second floor of the

Maywood, NJ distribution center. When Telling became the group manager, he had relocated the group offices to Maywood from the Sears fashion office in Manhattan.

I wore to the interview my one and only affordable wash-and-wear summer suit, an inexpensive suit I had purchased from the catalog two years prior. At the time, I wasn't aware that my modest suit might make a positive impression on the man from Danville, IL, Ed Telling, who was known to buy his own suits from Sears. Even so, I'm certain that Telling's suit was a far better quality than I could afford.

As I entered Telling's office, I was immediately impressed by the tall man that loomed up from behind his enormous desk. A smile stretched clear across his broad face, and my hand was enveloped by a much larger hand when we shook. For the first time in the presence of a "Giant of Industry" I was a little nervous. In person, I found Telling to be large in stature and personality.

Also present in the interview were key members of Telling's staff: William (Bill) Bass, the B stores manager (small stores), a dark haired and spectacled man of about my height and Bill Coon, the group's merchandise manager, who was almost as tall and rangy as Telling. The three men fit the description that one might expect of top company executives, and their casual discourse displayed a camaraderie that any corporation's team could wish for. I was told that Telling and Coon's homes were from the same neck of the woods in Danville, Illinois, "A couple of farms over," Coon added. Telling and Bass impressed me with their self-confidence and bearing, which must have been gained from their Sears' success and life-hardening experiences as WWII veterans. Telling, had been a Navy pilot and Bass, a decorated paratrooper.

We talked a little business, but sports turned up in the conversation, when I was asked if I had played sports. Looking at my 5'9" and 160 pound frame, they seemed surprised that I was a starting linebacker at West Philadelphia High school and a walk-on for University of Pennsylvania's freshman football team. This part of my resume seemed to inspire Telling to describe in sports terms how he meant to deal with a particular retail competitor. He laughed and shouted, "Kill Bubba kill!" Bubba Smith was Michigan State's two-time All American and was the country's best collegiate defensive end and famous for sacking quarterbacks. Telling's exclamation exemplified his philosophy toward his competitors: This leader didn't want to just beat his competition; he intended to crush them like the All American Bubba.

The interview's conversation became increasingly relaxed, and the session climaxed when Telling offering me the position as the New York Group's Division 200 Merchandise Manager. Still in need of greater income, supplied with a company car, and anxious to advance in the company's ranks, I didn't hesitate a second in accepting the position.

Weeks later, my first day on the job, I again met with Ed Telling, Bill Bass and Bill Coon where I committed my first blunder on the job, when I asked the Group Manager, "Mr. Telling, where would you like me to begin?"

Telling's eyebrows furrowed a bit, and a frowning shadow spread across that broad face. He leaned forward across his desk and said in a deep, hushed voice, "George, if I have to tell you what to do, I don't need you."

I gulped and said, "I'll get right to work." From that day on, I attempted to do exactly what Ed Telling wanted me to do, and I never again asked him what I should do.

My arrival in the New York Group was a time when regional catalog plant managers, like Bob Watson in Philadelphia, had a significant influence in retail markets - to Ed Telling's dismay. The catalog plant's catalog sales units were opened just a few miles from retail stores. Also, the plant had established central catalog telephone sales office units within a metropolitan market and directly competed with the retail stores by advertising their own 800 telephone numbers and making promotional calls into retail stores' areas.

The group's store managers attempted to excuse their own performance by griping to Telling about catalog units' overselling, stealing sales from their stores, and "having to eat catalog units' returns." Telling objected to Bob Watson's units' encroachment in the New York market, but he disliked even as much the excuses it provided his store managers.

It was the friction between Bob Watson and Ed Telling that led to my appointment. Telling held a deep resentment for the presence of central telephone sales offices and catalog sales offices within the New York Group's area, and Watson felt that Telling was stymying catalog growth in the huge New York market.

Telling was further annoyed by Watson's insistence that the New York group purchase substantially more catalogs to be mailed one-third deeper into the catalog index. Adding to Telling's irritations were letters from the plant's staff that chastised the group's stores for teletype order quality, excessive retail catalog returns, operating deficiencies, or other issues that were like annoying gnats and minutia to the group manager. Now that I was on the job, the dunning letters from Watson or his staff were forwarded to me.

The battle of titans was the toxic situation I walked into, and my retail-catalog management and catalog stores' experience was expected to smooth the feathers of both parties, the New York Group and the Catalog Plant. I would later learn that my salary was actually financed by Bob Watson, not the New York Group. Bob Watson had been so insistent to get the New York Group to improve its sales and operations that he was willing to pay my salary, and I imagine it was one of those offers that Telling couldn't refuse.

It was my understanding at the time that the catalog division still had influence in national headquarters under Chairman Kellstadt. By placating Watson and Kellstadt and assigning me as the group's catalog merchandise manager, it allowed Telling to concentrate on bigger and better things.

At the time, I had no way of knowing that Telling's resentment of catalog's influence in retail markets was just a prelude of the actions that he would take as he rose in positions of power. Telling's strategy of consolidating the New York group's retail stores' activities simmered with an ambition and a desire to carry his beliefs further and wider, and I couldn't imagine just how great a mark Telling was prepared to make at Sears. It was my good fortune that I found myself on the ground floor of a momentous shift in Sears' leadership and policies.

As one of the first steps in my new position I spent a couple of weeks accompanying Bill Bass through all of his B and C stores.

The stores classified as B stores were limited in soft-line merchandise offerings (clothing, linens, houseware), and the smaller C stores were primarily hard-lines (appliances, paint, hardware, home improvements).

My visits with Bass to his stores had some amusing highlights like our visit to a Queens C store. The store manager was a tall, fast talking, personable Italian-American. When he escorted Bass and me into his small telephone sales unit, we found only unmanned telephone positions and empty chairs in the room. Without skipping a beat, the store manager proceeded to provide a name for every chair and offered an excuse for the vacancy of each telephone salesperson's chair like "Mary called in sick this morning, and Charlotte is at lunch." I was rightly skeptical at the time and later learned that the telephone sales unit was rarely staffed, and the switchboard operator regularly performed triple-duty handling of retail store's communications, taking catalog customer inquiries, and writing catalog orders.

On my first visit with Bass to a C store in the heart of a relatively tough Bronx area, the store's manager proudly displayed in his office a gold painted brick. The brick had been thrown through the store's front window, and the store manager oddly felt that the brick was some sort of a trophy or a memento worthy of being painted gold. On a later visit to the golden brick store, I had been assigned to assist in the store's annual inventory. With a clipboard in hand I was in the midst of counting drill bits, when a disheveled man, reeking from cheap liquor or wine sidled up to me and slurred,

"I wanna buy a gun . . . I'm gonna shoot the bastard!"

"I'm sorry sir, but we don't sell firearms in this store."

"No guns! Damn! Then, I wanna buy a knife . . . I'll stab the son-a-bitch!"

The man staggered from the store unarmed.

I encountered similar experiences in our B store rounds, but there was one store that was a special case. The short, feisty store manager with a closely cropped, gray crew-cut was a unique character. Too often to the dismay of his catalog department's staff, the manager chose to man the catalog counter in disguise as a mere clerk, and he would regularly irritate customers by refusing to accept their returns of merchandise. When disgruntled customers asked to protest to the store manager, he wouldn't identify himself, but state that the manager wasn't in the store. He created a conundrum similar to the Major in the book and movie, *Catch 22*, when the Major was in, he was out.

During the height of my first Christmas season in the New York Group, the same B store manager displayed another one of his "quirks" where he avoided adding Division 200 staff to keep abreast of the increase in Christmas business by limiting the teletyping of multiple-item catalog orders to 100 per day, but the Christmas rush was producing about 200 or more multiple-item orders per day. It was obvious and untenable to me that the growing backlog of unprocessed customer orders had grown to a point that hundreds of customers wouldn't receive their orders in time for Christmas.

Even though I bore the catalog plant's criticism and the store manager's resentment, I carried a pile of unprocessed orders into the Philadelphia catalog plant to be entered into the order system. When the enormous shipment of backlogged orders arrived in the store's warehouse, I felt obligated to spend a full day assisting the store's catalog personnel in the sorting and packaging of customer orders. Despite the flak received from the catalog plant and the store manager, I was satisfied that many more of the store's catalog customers had a happier Christmas.

My main effort in the A stores, full-line merchandise stores, was devoted to improving sales and operational procedures and encouraging increased staff in the telephone sales units. With the opening of a New Jersey A store, I had the occasion to sit in on a review conducted by Telling with the new store manager. In my visits to the new store I had questioned the effectiveness of the division manager, but I was mostly disappointed that he hadn't been provided sufficient catalog divisional staff to complete the department's work.

In the new store's review, each member of the group's staff had the opportunity to critique his area of responsibility in the new store. When it was my turn to review the store's catalog department, I felt compelled to say to the store's manager, "The job simply isn't getting done, but if you're satisfied that you've given adequate support to your catalog manager, then I suggest you get another manager." My aim wasn't to displace the catalog manager, but only to stress the need for sufficient department staff.

If Telling wasn't in the room, I'm certain the store's manager might have attempted to strangle me, but Telling interrupted the store manager's response with more tactfully chosen words that dissuaded the manager's desire to kill me. From my contribution to the review session, Telling should have realized that he had appointed a catalog merchandise manager that wouldn't mince words, when a job needed to be done.

The group staff's job was hazardous, because it required considerable driving in super heavy traffic on the highways, streets, bridges, and tunnels to visit the New York group's stores. Even though I was a Philadelphia boy, who was familiar with the traffic snarls and hazards like Philadelphia's Schuylkill Expressway, fondly referred to by Philly's natives as "The Sure Kill Expressway," adjustment to heavy New York area traffic was difficult. I managed to reconcile myself to the fact that I was being paid to endure bumper to bumper traffic from my home and office in New Jersey, into the Holland and Lincoln tunnels, over the Cross

Bronx Expressway, the Long Island Expressway, and surrounding bridges.

On one wintery day in the Queens borough, it was late in the afternoon and I was attempting to visit several C stores, when my car hit a sheet of black ice beneath an underpass. I was suddenly alarmed to find my car had no traction, and the car began to slide uncontrollably toward an auto and bus stopped ahead at the light. I was forced to choose between a rear-end collision with the bus or automobile – I chose the bus. The company's car needed repair, but at least I avoided a more serious accident.

Another unhappy New York traffic experience occurred, when I was in a hurry to lead a meeting in the Brooklyn retail store where all the D/200 managers from Brooklyn, Queens and the Bronx had gathered. I became frustrated with the exceptional slow and heavy traffic in New Jersey. My frustration level increased as my car crawled through the Holland Tunnel and finally came to a complete stop on a ramp into Manhattan. After minutes ticked off with no movement on the ramp, I fumed each time I glared at my watch. Finally, I slammed the steering wheel a few times and decided I couldn't wait a minute longer. With a U turn back down the ramp, I hoped I could find another way into Manhattan. No luck - there was no other access into Manhattan, and all I could do was drive back into the Holland Tunnel, back to New Jersey.

Because I had no idea how I would be able to get back to the tunnel and on my way to Brooklyn, I panicked. Just as my car emptied out of the tunnel into New Jersey, with no idea how or when I could reverse course to Brooklyn, I instantly gave way to an irrational action and executed a U turn to head back through the tunnel.

A policeman standing ahead at the tunnel's mouth, who had just witnessed my incredibly stupid maneuver, displayed a combination of disgust and disbelief. The tunnel's guard scowled while waving me over with a vigorous chopping motion. Along with missing my meeting, I imagined all kinds of horrible things that were about to happen to me, like enormous fines and even jail time. Suddenly a divine revelation displaced my thought process. It had to be divine, because I pulled the car over to where the policeman stood, leaped out of the car, and threw my hands in the air and shouted, "Where am I?!"

The officer appeared to be stunned by my exclamation. He hesitated for a moment, walked up to me, placed his hand on my shoulder, and in the gentlest voice the officer asked, "Where ya tryin' to go fella?" I told him that I was lost and desperate to get to a meeting in Brooklyn. The officer proceeded to calmly tell me how to get to Brooklyn. I thanked the officer and resumed my journey.

When I finally walked into the Brooklyn store's meeting room, I was assailed with questions, "George where have you been?"

"I'm sorry, but it took me three trips through the Holland Tunnel to get here."

They thought I was kidding, but they should have known that nothing is impossible in travel in metropolitan New York.

As months passed I was challenged with resolving the most serious bones of contention between Telling and the catalog plant's general manager, Bob Watson. Entering the cross-fire between the two behemoths, I was handed all missiles of criticism hurled by Bob Watson and the catalog plant's staff. In response to the catalog plant's letters, that had irritated the hell out of my group manager, I promised corrective action. But I also rejected and countered some of the plant's attacks as unfounded, which might not have ingratiated me with Watson and his staff.

It wasn't long before I discovered that some of my disputes with the plant's complaints must not have gone over too well with Bob Watson and his staff. It was only an encounter with Charlie Moran, Eastern Territory's Operations Manager where I first realized the impact of some of my responses to the plant's complaints. After a few months on the job, I was eating lunch in the catalog plant's cafeteria, when Charlie Moran walked up to me. At this time, I knew of Charlie Moran, but I hadn't yet been introduced to him and I was surprised by his appearance.

"You're George Eaton, aren't you?"

"Yes sir."

"Please stand up for me for a minute."

I was incredulous, but I stood up.

"I just wanted to see, if you really have brass balls." With that said Moran walked away chuckling and left me standing a bit bewildered. I then realized that my counters to some of the plant's criticisms must have ruffled some feathers with Bob Watson and staff, but I didn't change my approach to their complaints.

As I worked to improve the group's catalog operations and defend the group from the catalog plant's more unfair critiques, I reported directly to Bill Coon, the New York Group's Merchandise Manager. I had little to no direct contact with Telling until he startled me one day, when he entered my office. Leaping to my feet, before I could even manage a hello, Telling put his huge hand on my shoulder and said, "George, keep doing what you're doing. You and I, we're standing shoulder to shoulder." Without another word he walked out of my office and left me agape with mixed feelings of surprise and satisfaction.

One of the most contentious issues that had stuck in Telling's craw was Bob Watson's demand that the New York Group purchase sufficient general catalogs (Big Book, the Spring and Fall catalogs) to mail one-third deeper into the catalog index. Telling had stubbornly resisted Watson's demand to invest in additional catalogs, but Watson continued to press Telling as I arrived on the scene.

Instead of a deeper mailing, I calculated that Telling might favor an approach that would benefit retail stores as well as catalog. I advised Telling that an increased mailing probably wouldn't get the biggest bang for the buck, because the deeper you delve into the lower levels of the index, the incidence increases of customers that are one-time shoppers, duplicate names, people that have moved, died, or bought too little, and not worth the investment in catalogs.

As an alternative to the deeper index mailing, I recommended that we buy the same number of additional catalogs proposed by the plant to support an offer that would put catalogs in the hands of better retail and catalog customer prospects.

Because Revolving Charge credit customers were among Sears best customers, I suggested that catalogs in retail and catalog credit customers' hands would be far more productive than customers in the catalog index's second tier. Printed on Revolving Charge credit customer statements would be an offer to pick up a free catalog at their nearest Sears store.

Telling accepted my proposal, because he agreed that there should be an advertising advantage to retail stores as well, if more Sears Revolving Charge customers had catalogs to pre-shop retail. Bob Watson reluctantly agreed to the New York Group's proposal, even though he didn't get exactly what he wanted, he realized that he still would achieve greater catalog penetration in an important New York market.

CATALOG DISTRIBUTION AND CATALOG-RETAIL SYNERGISM

As a result of introducing additional catalogs into the New York market and offering free catalogs to Sears Revolving Charge customers, New York Group's retail stores were engulfed by credit customers' demands for free catalogs and significant increases in retail and catalog sales were realized. This only confirmed what numerous studies had consistently established that retail customers pre-shopped retail through the catalog, and it was simply logical that a catalog in the hands of a Sears Revolving Charge customer, customers with better credit ratings, was a superior investment for the retail and

catalog business than mailing a catalog to a marginal or non-existent catalog customer.

About a year later, the group's controller stopped me to say, "I believe that your plan to offer catalogs to revolving charge customers was part of the group's success last year." I was pleasantly surprised at this endorsement, but it was a logical conclusion. This should have had national implications, but the opportunity to employ this catalog distribution strategy arose years later, but was never again implemented.

Another thorny issue arose, when telephone centralization advocates confronted Telling and tried to convince him that all stores should centralize their telephone sales activities into a large New York telephone central unit. Telling and my objections to telephone centralization were not exactly the same, but we were convinced that every store should have its own telephone sales unit.

Telling's position was influenced by his objection to the catalog plant's invasion of Telephone Sales Offices into the New York market, but his most important reason to oppose centralization was his conviction that every store should stand on its own and be judged accordingly. He had his fill of his store managers complaining about sales and returns intrusions by catalog stores and catalog telephone sales offices, realizing he'd probably receive the same complaints and excuses related to the group's own telephone central unit. Telling asked me to develop a "white paper" that stressed the importance of telephone units in every store in comparison to the negatives related to telephone centralization.

TELEPHONE SALES CENTRALIZATION

Because I realized the value of a strong telephone sales force in each of my previous four stores, I readily endorsed Telling's opposition to telephone centralization. In summary, my position paper argued that a store with its own telephone sales unit realized a greater emphasis on the development of catalog sales, improved accountability on the prevention of catalog returns, enhanced a store's involvement in efficient catalog operations, and bettered store's identity in its market. Telling accepted my report and used it to support his opposition to centralization. He must have won this battle versus proponents of centralization, because Telling didn't broach the subject again

until years later. However, this was to be only the opening salvo for retail-minded factions that might press for telephone centralization.

Another contentious issue was the demand by the Catalog Plant and the Territory's D/200 Merchandise Manager to promotionally call the New York Group's entire catalog distribution index. To justify the plant's plan to promotionally call all customers, even customers with a lower purchasing history, statistics from a promotional call study was offered.

The promotional call study indicated customers in the lower levels of the index when promotionally called purchased a greater percentage in number of sales than customers promotionally called in the higher levels of the index.

Applying simple mathematics, I pointed out that even though when promotionally called, customers in the top levels of the index may have resulted in a smaller percentage in number of sales improvement than the lower portion of the index, the value of the upper tier customer purchased more annually and their greater value should produce more in dollars in sales as shown in the hypothetical example below:

Customers When Promotionally Called

Example:

A $100 customer bought 5% more in number of orders or $5 more.

A $25 customer bought 10% more in number of orders or $2.50 more.

PROMOTIONAL CALLING

In the active promotional call programs in the telephone units of all the stores I managed, I was convinced that promotional calling produced additional sales. The most successful promotional calling programs were calls to preferred customer lists where telephone salespersons established appointments with customers to call back when customers had time to prepare their orders for key shopping periods like Easter, Back to School, Early Shoppers Discount, and Christmas. Customers generally took the time to build larger orders in anticipation of being called back on appointments.

After refuting the claim that customers in the lower level of the index were more productive when called, instead of promotional calling the entire customer index, I convinced the Catalog Plant to only mail customer lists to New York Group stores that consisted of customers in the top 1/3 of the index. I maintained that a focus on the highest value customers would help make promotional calling produce greater sales at a lower cost and minimize store managers' opposition to this particular payroll investment.

Some argued that promotional calling was ineffective and resented by customers, but my experience had proven to me that effective salespeople were able to cultivate relationships with their customers to produce increased sales and the use of down times on incoming calls should allow time to make promotional calls. In following years, the value of promotional calling had to be defended vigorously, but the battle was eventually lost because retail store managers failed to recognize the benefit of effective promotional calling and withheld the hours that might be needed to make promotional calls.

Only months into my New York Group assignment, the group office was relocated into the new Willowbrook store in Wayne, NJ. About the time of our relocation, Territory and National D/200 Merchandise Managers visited the New York Group, and I was happy to have the opportunity to show the actions I had taken to build the group's catalog business. Ed Telling and the National D/200 Merchandise Manager knew each other well, and I believed that their relationship was good until the national manager made a P&L presentation to the group's Division 200 managers in a conference room down the hall from Telling's office.

The national manager chose to describe Division 200's importance to a store's profitability by reviewing a store's Profit and Loss statement, line by line, to show how the catalog business contributed to a retail store's profit. I'm not sure who informed Telling about the P&L presentation, but Telling was outraged when he heard of it. Telling didn't believe that an examination of the company's profit and loss statement was appropriate for division managers, especially not Division 200 managers. Up to this point, Telling had been very supportive of my efforts to improve the catalog business, but the P&L exposure to our D/200 managers was a bridge too far for him.

As months went by, I observed that the group staff genuinely liked and respected Ed Telling. Any time I was in Bill Coon's office and Telling appeared, Bill would leap to his feet - he was out the door to beat a path to the boss. In the ensuing years, no matter who I was with, everything would stop on Telling's appearance, because Telling rarely joined a meeting, but expected immediate attention by his lieutenants. Just his appearance meant, "See me at once!"

Because Telling had elevated his staff to transfer from store managers their decision making in merchandising, operating, advertising, and display, some store managers resented their diminished stature and the group staff's interference. This lost influence was felt and resented most by the veteran store managers, especially the A store managers that had been kings of their domains for years prior to Telling's arrival.

On a visit to one of the older New Jersey's A stores, the veteran store manager leaned back in his chair behind his impressive desk as I pitched the importance of adequately staffing his catalog department. He was expressionless throughout my presentation, but before I could finish my list of recommendations, the old pro lifted a hand up to interrupt my spiel, leaned toward me over his desk, looked me straight in the eye, and said in a fatherly tone, "What's a nice guy like you doing in a dirty job like this?" I was pretty sure the question was rhetorical and he didn't expect an answer.

The veteran manager simply expressed the frustration of other long-time store managers that had been stripped of much of their authority and prestige by Telling, because he like other store managers resented the feeling of Telling's influence on visits by the group's operating and merchandising staff.

In 1967, Gordon Metcalf was named Chairman of Sears and Ed Telling was promoted to Vice President of the Eastern Territory. The entire New York Group staff and every store manager attended a big farewell party to celebrate Telling's promotion. Telling received various gifts from those present and most of the gifts were meant to be amusing and provoked belly laughs from those in attendance.

Because I didn't think a little sketch that I had drawn was good enough, I lost my nerve to present to Telling a framed cartoon in which I had drawn of two people standing outside Ed Telling's office. One said to the other, "Heck, Ed Telling puts his pants on just like you and I." Inside the office, my cartoon depicted Telling suspended in air as two winged angels were pulling his pants up. To this day, I regret that I didn't present to Telling my rough piece of art at the party. I believe everyone would have gotten a kick out of it, especially Telling.

CHAPTER SEVEN
ED BRENNAN

Shortly after Telling's move to the Eastern Territory Vice President's office, Bill Coon and I joined the territory's staff, Bill as the territory's Merchandise Manager and I became the territory's Division 200 Merchandise Manager. Bill Bass had been assigned as store manager for the new White Plains, NY store, and he was replaced by Ed Brennan, a store manager from the Midwest Territory.

Brennan had started with Sears as a sales associate in Madison, WI, a 3rd generation Sears' employee. His grandfather had worked with the company's founder, Richard Sears, and his uncles and brothers were buyers with the company. Politically savvy associates opined that Brennan's appearance in the New York Group was significant and surmised that the newcomer was on the so-called "fast track" and destined for bigger and better things. They were proven correct only thirteen years later when he became chairman of the Merchandise Group.

My New York Group Division 200 Merchandise Manager's position had been capably filled by Rus Munzer, who I had recommended as the group's strongest catalog division manager. Rus held Ed Brennan in high regard, and in turn he benefited from Brennan's support. The relationship between Rus and Brennan was evident during the New York group's sponsorship of a large and elaborate promotional meeting for the group's D/200 managers and telephone unit managers. The audience was entertained by a first-rate fashion show with professional models, exciting merchandise and marketing presentations by top notch national merchants, and everyone was feted with a well catered luncheon.

Not to be outshined by this professional and comprehensive show presented by an assemblage of some of the best headquarters' merchants, Ed Brennan took the stage. Even before he began to speak, his audience had to be impressed by the tall, youthful, and handsome executive. Brennan proceeded to wow the crowd with a glowing tribute to Catalog and described its vital role in the corporation. Brennan's address to the group extolled Catalog's contribution to the company in such adulatory terms his speech might have been made by Catalog's vice president.

Russ turned to me and gushed, "Isn't he terrific . . . and he's only 40!"

While I was impressed and appreciated Brennan's speech and admired the terrific meeting the New York Group had organized, I meekly looked for a bit of credit for my contribution to the meeting and said, "Yeah Rus, I agree. By the way, you know I'm 40 too."

Rus didn't respond, wasn't impressed, or he didn't hear me over the crowd's cheers. He heard me.

After a couple of years, Ed Brennan confirmed that he was still "on track," when he was promoted to the Western New York Group's manager's position. In my first visit to Brennan's office in Buffalo, NY, our meeting was attended by Mike Bozic, the group's young operating manager. In 1987, less than 20 years after this meeting, Bozic became President and CEO of the Sears Merchandise Company. In this meeting the junior Bozic sat attentively and silently at one side of Brennan's desk, while I did my best to absorb Brennan's litany on how the catalogs should be better merchandised.

Brennan immediately made it clear that he had specific ideas on how Catalog's approach to merchandising needed correction. He began his critique with, "Here - I'll show you what I mean!" With that, he threw open a Spring general catalog (The Big Book) onto his desk and began to furiously leaf through the pages. He would pause on a page, spin the catalog around, point to an item and declare, "There, that's what I mean!" Then he would express his detailed opinions on how Catalog's merchandising approach should be modified or limited in certain ways and how the catalog's merchants should better coordinate with retail's merchants.

Brennan didn't stop with the general catalog and continued his merchandising lesson by going over several Specialized catalogs and a couple of monthly flyers. I did my best to keep up with all the theories that Brennan espoused. I nodded even when I didn't fully understand or agree, but during our hour-long conversation Brennan troubled me when he went on further to describe the current friction between the retail and catalog divisions as a "War".

At least in my mind, I felt our differences in Catalog's role at Sears were professional and should be cooperative and amicable. I could only hope that we weren't really antagonists involved in some kind of a war. As I left Brennan's office, I reflected on Telling's catalog concerns that I had confronted, but had come to understand and appreciate where my boss and I stood on the issues most important to Catalog. But Brennan's depiction of retail and catalog differences as an equivalent to a war left me concerned.

Coincidentally, shortly after Brennan moved on to become the Boston Group Manager, I happened upon a story in Time magazine. The article featured a picture of a dazed Japanese soldier, who had just emerged from the jungle in Guam thirty years after the end of World War II. Because the Japanese soldier was unaware of the war's end, I thought I could playfully connect the dazed soldier's appearance to Brennan's "war" comment. I addressed a note to Brennan and attached the Time's article with a note of appreciation for his continued cooperation and asked, "Is the war over?" Brennan responded amicably in keeping with the spirit of my letter, but over the following years and events I could only hope that

Brennan didn't still harbor the belief that an actual "war" existed between the retail and catalog divisions.

One of Telling's first actions as the territory's vice president was to close the Boston catalog plant and service the Boston region from Philadelphia's catalog plant. In conjunction with closing the Boston plant, the vice president made another surprising move by naming Hank Sunderland, the Boston catalog plant's operating superintendent, as his Administrative Assistant.

Sunderland began his career in June 1952 in the Los Angeles Catalog Merchandise Distribution Center and his appointment marked a new direction for catalog in the Eastern Territory. Telling wanted an experienced catalog plant operator to implement the addition of service to the Boston region by the Philadelphia catalog plant and initiate cost savings in the process. It didn't take Sunderland long before the Philadelphia plant's next day delivery service was discontinued.

ELIMINATION OF NEXT DAY DELIVERY

With Sunderland's catalog operations' credentials and Telling's support, the Philadelphia plant's Next Day Delivery

service was discontinued. Next Day Service had announced to the customer that an order placed before noon today could be picked up by the following afternoon. Special signing in stores promoted the fact: *An order placed by noon today will be ready for pickup after 3pm tomorrow.* The expedited service required commitment by the selling units transmitting orders to the catalog plant before the next-day cut-off, catalog plant's processing of orders on the next day schedule, trucking companies reaching the stores in time to fulfill the next day promise to customers, and the stores processing orders to meet the pickup time promised.

The decision to discontinue Next Day Service allowed the plant to eliminate a shift each work day, made the plant's operations more effective, and trucking companies were not held to as tight a shipping schedule. The catalog selling units were relieved of the pressure to teletype next-day orders by the necessary cut-off, and on the following day they were relieved of the pressure to process incoming plant shipments in time for customer pick-up by 3pm.

The plant's labor cost savings were measurable, but the impact on sales and returns were not. When I was informed of the decision to end next day service, I was disappointed that I wasn't advised before the decision was made. There was no consideration given to how much customers' purchase decisions were based on the next day service. Even though unclaimed orders were a significant percentage of total customer returns, reduced service's impact on returns was ignored. There was sufficient evidence that the quicker a store was able to deliver an order for the customer, the less likely the order would be unclaimed by the customer.

In today's marketing, it deserves to be noted that Amazon, the internet's dominant merchandiser, has clearly recognized the value of improved customer service as noted in a series of news articles:

The Street's September 2015 article – Amazon's plan to expand its one-hour delivery.

New York Times, December 14, 2016 – Amazon's CEO announced its first drone delivery to England.

Seattle Times January 11, 2016 – Amazon poised to take on UPS/FEDX in deliveries due to its prioritization of service.

To neglect the importance of customer service simply in the quest for cost savings is a false choice, if greater merchandise sales and fewer customer returns is your goal. Amazon seems to understand that, but the company's officers often failed to take that into account.

Another major change in the Eastern Territory began with a request for me to accompany an entourage that included Telling, Sunderland, and Coon to meet with retail's Northeast Zone management. The Northeast Zone encompassed the areas of New England and northern New York State. The purpose of the meeting was to decide the disposition of the Northeast Zone's retail satellites, like the satellite I had managed in Alexandria, VA.

At the time, each retail satellite was administered by a retail store and incorporated in the store's Profit and Loss statement (P&L), just as my satellite's financials were embodied in the Alexandria, VA's retail store. Telling abhorred the idea of any store's performance being buried in another unit's P&L. Telling held a strong conviction that even the smallest store should stand on its own merit, and a retail store should be judged without a satellite's influence.

At the Northeast Zone meeting Telling asked me, if I should take over the administration of all the zone's retail satellites. Instead of accepting Telling's proposal, I recommended that the Zone office should establish district managers like the CSO organization, and the retail satellites in each district should be converted to catalog and appliances stores as free standing units. When advertising was addressed, I pointed out that the catalog media was dominant in the smaller catalog and appliance stores' markets, and advertising should remain catalog oriented and not incorporated into retail markets' advertising.

The day after the meeting, Bill Coon told me that I should have jumped at Telling's offer. This became evident, when Dick Lamb rose to the occasion and presented a plan to Telling that covered the entire Eastern Territory. Lamb rightly feared that Telling may have been prepared to replace the entire CSO organization with a complete takeover by retail. Lamb's regional plan transferred CSOs closest to retail markets to retail control, but kept all other CSOs within the regional CSO administration. Telling bought Lamb's restructure plan, Lamb kept much of his organization, and retail groups absorbed catalog units within their stores' markets. Even though I turned down an opportunity to participate in a major structural change, I believed then and now my position was a fair compromise and the most effective approach at the time.

In 1971, I traveled to Columbus, Ohio to visit the newly opened state of the art distribution center, the Columbus Catalog Merchandise Distribution Center (CMDC) opened with a fully mechanized fashion distribution center designed to distribute nationally fashion merchandise that was most vulnerable to returns.

Much of the merchandise consisted of items like dresses, suits, and shoes, items that experienced high returns and liquidation losses due to fit and style issues. I was impressed by the building that looked like an enormous dry cleaners. The state of the art systems were designed to accommodate at minimal cost all forms of soft line merchandise from gowns to boxes. The Columbus plant left me with a glow of pride and a feeling that the company was prepared to make the investments necessary to improve catalog's profitability now and into the future.

On the job in the following months, I kept myself busy by addressing ways in which I could make Division 200 more effective in order to engender greater support from retail store management. My management experience in stores and the group taught me that it was essential that catalog divisions were adequately staffed to permit good customer service at the counter, storage area, and telephone room in order to maximize sales and minimize returns.

In the ensuing months as the territory's Division 2OO merchandise manager, I took the opportunity to study man hours required in each activity with the goal to develop a guideline for payroll planning. The resultant Division 200 Payroll Planner was designed to incorporate productivity standards based on catalog order volume. Productivity standards included number of hours required to receive shipments, pack and bin orders, and orders packed per hour. Numbers of hours required for counter and telephone staff were based on sales volume.

Not long after I completed my studies and finished the payroll planner, Al Stewart, one of Charlie Moran's young and able operating assistants, appeared in my office. Al informed me that Moran had directed him to accompany me in store visits to measure the effectiveness of the payroll planner. Little did I realize how much my career would be influenced by Al Stewart, who would become my boss, and in 1993 he would be named President of Full-Line Sears Stores.

Al and I visited a number of Vermont and New Hampshire stores in the Northeast Zone. As a result of our store visits, Al agreed that my payroll planner should be useful and offer reasonable payroll guidance to all Division 200 units in retail and catalog and appliance stores.

With good payroll guidance sufficient man hours would allow adequate sales force to service customers and improve operations to control returns. In addition the D/200 Payroll Planner helped make retail management feel more confident that their catalog department could be as accountable and efficient as any other retail division.

But just when I believed I was on the right track, there arose a major bump in the road. Bill Coon and I met the bump in something called special orders.

SPECIAL ORDERS

As much as I was confident that Telling supported my efforts in the improvement of catalog activities, he had his limitations. One of those limitations reared up, when Bill Coon and I met with members of headquarters' catalog marketing staff. They proposed a Special Order program that would place cut pages from the Big Book (general catalog) into the respective hardlines' retail departments to permit employees to place Special Orders from cut catalog pages, when customers couldn't find desired items in the retail departments.

The Special Order program would augment the stores' current red phone kiosks and signage that were positioned in a number of locations in the retail stores. The kiosk had an array of catalogs mounted on a shelf. A red phone was mounted on the kiosk to allow a customer to place an order directly with the store's telephone sales unit.

Bill and I believed that a Special Order program had the potential for improved customer satisfaction, increased sales, and satisfied a desire to cooperate with the headquarters' proposal. We set in motion the purchase of many hundreds of binders, and the creation of many thousands of cut catalog pages to supply all of the Eastern territory's retail stores.

The binders were to be placed in hard-lines retail departments with their appropriate catalog merchandise pages. Signage would direct the customers to ask a salesperson, if they were unable to find what they wanted. The retail salesperson would refer the customer to the binder's catalog pages and use the department's phone to call the customer's order into the telephone unit.

Just days before the binders and cut pages were about to be shipped to the stores, I was surprised to look up to see Bill Coon enter my office with a strange expression on his face. He occasionally would visit my office, but it was the look on his face that made me sit up to hear him say,

"George, Telling got wind of the Special Order program and told me to kill it."

"That's it." With that said Bill spun around and began to walk out.

I stammered, "But what will we do with all the binders and catalog pages?"

Not turning, Bill said over his shoulder, "Don't worry. I'll handle it."

It surprised me that Coon hadn't thought to advise Telling of the Special Order plan, because Coon had a good sense of Telling's beliefs. Even though it may have been a reasonable approach to keep disappointed customers from walking, the two of us should have realized that the program ran contrary to Telling's view of Catalog's role within a retail store and considered red phone kiosks in retail stores were an intrusion in a store's design.

Telling believed catalog had its place and a retail store's merchandising should be retail store personnel's primary concern. He maintained that if retail salespeople leaned on

catalog merchandise offerings, they wouldn't focus on their basic retail merchandising responsibilities like being in-stock, offering an alternative to their customers, and trading up to a better product.

We had to appreciate Telling's pragmatic approach to the retail business, but now Bill Coon was charged to find some use for a ton of unused binders.

The year 1973 marked the opening of the Sears Tower, 110 stories, 1,454 feet high, and Arthur Wood was tapped as Chairman. For the first time, I along with the other Territories Division 200 Merchandise Managers from Atlanta (South), Dallas (Southwest), Chicago (Midwest), Los Angeles (West) met together for the first time in headquarters. Before our invitations to Chicago only the regional catalog plant managers and their CSO staff had been afforded the opportunity to visit headquarters to provide input to the headquarters' catalog marketing and merchandising staffs. New stature had been given to my counterparts and me, and I suspect that Telling had influenced our recognition in headquarters.

With little fanfare, Telling was named Vice President of the Midwest Territory, but it was merely a brief stopover before his attainment of the highest corporate positions. A year later, Telling headed a new headquarters office, Department 702, as Senior Executive Vice President Field. Almost immediately, Hank Sunderland left the East to lead Telling's catalog responsibilities in Department 702C. Sunderland's new department was designed to head all field catalog operations.

In one swift move Telling had taken control of all field operations and entrusted his man, Sunderland to make Catalog more like retail. One of the more subtle changes was the status of the regional catalog plant managers, who once were treated like vice presidents on their visits to headquarters, and now their position was reduced as comparable to managers of large retail distribution centers.

While Telling and Sunderland had assumed their powerful positions on the 68th floor of the Sears Tower, I was busy preparing for the important 1976 Back to School season. With the help of Philadelphia's D/200 Merchandise Manager, Jim Curran, a slide and voice presentation was developed that outlined the steps needed by the stores' Division 200 managers to promote Back to School sales and operate efficiently during an important catalog shopping season.

On Sunderland's return visit to the Eastern Territory's St. David's office, he stopped by my office to discuss my view on catalog priorities. During our lengthy discussion, I mentioned that I had recently completed a Back to School slide presentation that outlined operating and merchandising strategies to maximize Division 200 effectiveness in the important back to school shopping season. Sunderland asked to see the slide show, and after viewing the presentation he expressed his appreciation and his surprise that it was my voice that performed the commentary throughout.

My London born and Latin teacher mother, who still retained a cultured English accent, chastised me plenty for mumbling or not speaking distinctly enough. But when I recorded the commentary on the video I had done my best to articulate each word as clearly as I could, and I think my elocution in the slide show might have been greeted by a smile on my dear departed mother's face.

It was only a few weeks later I learned that my Back to School presentation impressed Sunderland more than I realized.

CHAPTER EIGHT
THE SEARS TOWER

In the eight years that had passed on the Eastern Territory's staff, my job had become routine in travels to stores throughout the territory, and I had too much time on evenings and weekends to improve my tennis game and coach my two sons in little league football - I was ready for a change.

Change finally came during my annual meeting of the territory's group and zone Division 200 merchandise managers. The session was interrupted when my secretary entered the meeting room to tell me that Mr. Sunderland from Chicago was on the phone. My reaction was swift. I immediately excused myself from the meeting and raced up to my office. When Sunderland invited me to Chicago to discuss an assignment as his new department's National Division 200 Manager, I indicated that I'd be happy to join him.

Upon my flight's arrival at Chicago's O'Hare airport, a taxi took me to the tallest building in the world. I had been to a few marketing meetings in the Sears Tower, but this visit was very special - I was about to be interviewed for a national position. The thought of a promotion and change made my steps a lot bouncier into the building and to the elevators. Two elevator rides were required to reach the corporate offices on the Tower's 68th floor where I was escorted into Henry Sunderland's office.

I noted that Sunderland's office was next to SEVP Telling's office. Sunderland outlined his field staff's impressive mission to provide national direction for all sales and operating activities of the selling units and distribution centers. I was offered the position of National Division 200 (retail catalog) Manager.

During my interview with Sunderland, I caught glimpses of Telling whisk by Sunderland's door. At one point, Sunderland must have received a particular signal, leaped from his chair, and pursued his chief. This wasn't unlike the way in which Telling summoned his staff back in New York and the Eastern Territory. Back from his short session with Telling, Sunderland asked for my decision, and I immediately accepted the offer to join his headquarters' staff.

The field's catalog selling unit staff was led by Jim Goodwin, National Catalog Selling Unit Manager and included National Managers for D/200 (retail catalog), CSO (catalog sales offices),

CSM (catalog sales merchants and agents), and Catalog Plant Merchandising.

Our staff's offices were on the 68th floor, where the company's highest executives' offices were located and just steps away from Sunderland and Telling's offices. As Telling and Sunderland's representatives, our staff would have significant influence on the field and headquarters. Each one of us on the selling unit staff was charged to establish concrete objectives that would achieve uniformity and efficiencies in all catalog operations and merchandising. The department's catalog priorities were backed by Telling and Sunderland and our influence reverberated throughout the Tower and field units.

Much of what my associates on the 702C staff worked on was putting all of the regions' Catalog stores (CSOs), Merchants (CSMs), and Agents (CSAs), catalog plants, and merchandise management on the same page. Sunderland focused on plant operations and expansion of the catalog plants' physical space to better handle retail distribution. **Unfortunately, because retail later would extract their inventories from catalog plants into**

retail distribution centers, this expansion of catalog plant facilities became additional overhead costs that could impact the catalog division's profitability.

Another 702C staff member, Dave Maakestad, who had been a merchandise manager in the Philadelphia catalog plant and a very good tennis player, was primarily charged to expand and nationalize an outlet store program.

My very first task was to evaluate a catalog order entry system (COE) that was in a laboratory development stage in Louisville, KY. Members of a very capable operating staff headed by Jim Harvison accompanied me on a flight to Louisville on a company plane. On my very first visit to Louisville, I recognized immediately the numerous advantages offered by the COE system: When a salesperson entered the customer's order into a desktop CRT monitor, the system electronically verified all aspects of the order and transmitted the order to the catalog plant.

The COE system instantly verified customer name, address, and credit account number against customer data on file that helped eliminate customer duplications and improved the accuracy in customer evaluation and catalog media distribution. The credit account number and account status enabled accuracy in input and an instant credit check. The entry of catalog item information and stock availability information was verified, which substantially reduced order entry errors and allowed customers an option to select another item when informed of out of stock or delay issues.

As soon as the operating and system staffs concluded that the COE system was operationally ready, I accepted the system enthusiastically and suggested to Sunderland that the COE system was ready to be tested in the stores, and Sunderland asked me to prepare a presentation to Telling. Later in a formal presentation to Telling and Sunderland, with the aid of visuals, I outlined the COE system's operational efficiencies and economics and proposed a full test in one metropolitan market in each of the five territories. At the conclusion of my presentation, Telling smiled and nodded to Sunderland. Telling's nod was enough for Sunderland, and I was directed to get started on the tests' implementations.

With the assistance of the operations and systems personnel, all retail units in five metropolitan markets were equipped with the order entry system. Over the following twelve months, the COE system was operational in the five test markets.

The five market tests required a number of follow-up visits and collection of data to measure results of the test markets compared to prior year performance and in relation to other markets without the COE advantage.

At the conclusion of the COE test, the results met all expectations and based on my recommendation to Sunderland, Telling approved the program's roll-out nationally. Telling's acceptance of a national roll-out of the COE system was satisfying, but more importantly it represented an advancement toward a major improvement in Catalog's operational efficiency and enhanced customer service.

Telling and Sunderland accompanied me to our first roll-out meeting in the Midwest Territory's Chicago office. We proposed the order entry system's implementation in all of the territory's retail stores where the COE system would be placed in all Division 200 telephone units and counters. During my presentation to the Midwest territory's staff, one staff member spoke up and suggested that it might be more cost effective to have the COE system installed in a Chicago central telephone unit rather than the telephone sales units in all stores.

To tell the truth I would have done anything to get the COE system installed anywhere, but before I could respond Telling broke in and made it clear that the COE system was not designed to facilitate the initiation of central telephone units. He reiterated the same points that I had given him in opposition to centralization years prior. Telling continued on to make it clear to the Midwest Territory that every store should have its own telephone sales unit and the COE system should be installed at every catalog counter and every telephone sales desk. From that point on every territory received the same message.

By 1978, COE territory roll-out presentations had gone well, Telling was named Chairman, Sunderland was promoted to Vice President of the Pacific Coast Territory, Jim Goodwin went with Sunderland as the territory's Catalog Manager, and I was promoted to replace Jim Goodwin as the National Catalog Selling Unit Manager under Jack Kelly, Vice President of Catalog.

Because the COE rollout had been accepted by all the other territories with the exception of the Southern territory, my new boss, Jack Kelly accompanied me to the Southern Territory's office in Atlanta to meet with the territory's new Vice President, Ed Brennan. Brennan had been the Boston Group Manager since 1977. Unfortunately, Brennan wasn't sufficiently swayed by Telling's support for the COE program or the efficiencies in catalog operations that would be created. He described all the economy measures he had initiated upon taking command of the Southern territory, and an investment in installing the COE system at that time would be contrary to his current program to cut costs. Brennan asked us to delay the roll-out in his territory, though he recognized the potential advantages of the order entry system.

Jack Kelly and I walked out of Brennan's office disappointed. Even though we could understand Brennan's efforts to sell his cost cutting program in the territory and how COE's implementation might run counter to his territory's cost cutting strategy, I wished that Brennan could have prioritized the benefit to Catalog. .

Following the order entry's roll-out, that eventually included the Southern territory; I aimed to proceed to the customer merchandise returns phase of the COE system. Conceptually, a customer's catalog returned item would be identified to the original order and be entered into the COE returns system at the selling unit. The entire paperwork trail and accounting process would replace the current burdensome manual system with the mechanized creation of the customer's return transaction and shipping documentation and electronically transmit data to process merchandise, adjust inventory, and reconcile accounting in the plant and selling unit.

The current method to process returns was work intensive in the stores and the catalog plants, as well as an accounting nightmare. The COE returns system would electronically save the stores and catalog plants many thousands of man hours and significantly improve accuracy in paperwork, accounting and inventory. My effort to have the system developed and installed was frustrated for years. My vigorous support of the returns system's implementation eventually led to my experiencing a number of stone walls. There were always other corporate interests that received higher priority in system development, and my hopes for initiation of the COE returns system remained on the shelf.

Frustrated by inaction on the returns system, I moved on to pursue other ways to reduce catalog payroll costs and improve efficiency in retail stores that included Self- Service Pickup. Instead of an employee retrieving smaller bin packages, a customer-friendly bin area was designed to allow the customer to retrieve easily carried packages. Larger items continued to be delivered to the customer by a counter employee. Customers appeared to accept the self-service system, because they felt self-service offered them quicker service. The stores needed fewer counter personnel, but accomplished better service to more customers in less time.

Continuing in my quest to make catalog operations more cost efficient, I challenged our systems people to find a company that could produce an automatic calling system that would advise customers that their packages were available for pickup. The task of calling customers to tell them that their orders were ready for pickup was work intensive, but an essential activity to preserve sales by reducing the number of orders not picked up. When sufficient man-hours weren't provided to make the necessary pickup calls, unclaimed orders could be as much as 20 percent or more of a unit's total orders.

At the time, hotels had systems to generate wakeup calls, but there was nothing we could find in the industry that could produce a device that was capable of making hundreds of daily calls accompanied by a pickup message. After a number of months the systems team discovered a Florida company that had developed a "breadboard model" calling system. The so-called "breadboard model" allowed the entry of a large list of customers' telephone numbers into the prototype. When a voice response was detected, an "Order ready for pickup" message was initiated. A few months later the calling machine evolved into a mass produced model and was rolled out into the stores.

The automated calling device had the potential to save thousands of man hours in the selling units and significantly reduce unclaimed orders. Unfortunately, similar technology has been advanced today to barrage homes with political and advertising messages.

Some of the most fun times I had on the job were visits to groups and stores in the territories. Some of the field sessions were connected to the introduction of the COE system, marketing plans, and operating issues, but the meetings could be varied based on the locale: Highlights of Dallas' lively catalog meetings were the loud playing of a song's refrain, *"You can take this job and shove it!"*, along with tasty servings of sausage and biscuit sandwiches.

From my very first meeting in the New York group and subsequent meetings, I believed its catalog people to be the most aggressive, knowledgeable and challenging group in the entire Sears nation. When I returned from Chicago to face the entire group of division managers and their telephone managers to introduce the COE system, as a joke I controlled the boisterous meeting with a whip and a whistle.

In addition to the opportunity to meet many of the great Sears people in the stores and the catalog plants, a perk in my travels was the introduction to superb and unique regional foods like salmon in Seattle, Fajitas in San Diego, Gumbo in New Orleans, Paella in Miami, Scrod in Boston, and frog legs in Brownsville, TX. In one visit where I may have offended my Texan hosts, when I held up a frog's fried limb and stated, "I'm sorry, you may say that frog legs taste like chicken, but I can't ignore the fact that so many frogs were sacrificed for their legs, when I'd just as soon have chicken."

The time I served on the national field staff, from 1976 to 1980, was the most productive, rewarding and successful period of my entire career at Sears, because with few obstacles and great support from the operating, systems and marketing staffs I was able to contribute to the accomplishment of major programs that had national significance toward the advancement of Catalog's sales and operational efficiencies.

CHAPTER NINE
REORGANIZATION

The year 1978 marked the beginning of significant changes in company policies and direction. Telling had been appointed Chairman and Philip J. Purcell, who had led McKinsey consultants' study of Sears, was named Senior Vice President of Corporate Administrative Planning. Restructuring moves were announced with the conversion of Catalog Merchandise Distribution Centers from profit centers to cost centers like any other distribution center in the company's logistics network. This served to deemphasize catalog's influence and just another brick removed from Catalog's corporate stature.

Other actions included the New York fashion office in Manhattan move to 2 N Lasalle Street in Chicago. Personally, the fashion center's move from Manhattan offered me the opportunity to have my picture taken with super model Cheryl Tiegs, when she visited the fashion departments' new Chicago offices. Cheryl had become famous from her appearance on the front cover of *Sports Illustrated's* 1978 swimsuit issue.

A line of Cheryl Tieg's clothing was about to be introduced by Sears and featured in retail stores and in catalogs. Cheryl impressed me as personable and pretty in person as she appeared in a swimsuit on *Sports Illustrated's* front cover, and she later appeared on the front cover of the 1984 Spring and Summer catalog. Over the years luminaries like Ted Williams, legendary baseball hall of famer and actor Vincent Price had been contracted to endorse and feature Sears products.

The year's changes impacted all of Sears, not just the catalog division. It appeared to me that management's concern for employee dedication and loyalty took a back seat for the corporation's desire to impress Wall Street and improve the company's stock price. My conversation with a national manager exemplified a change in corporate attitude toward its employees when he described a policy change that I believed would be unfavorably received by employees. When I indicated that such a change wouldn't sit well with employees, he professed that jobs were currently scarce and employees would settle for the change, if they wanted to keep their job. Until that time I hadn't heard and wouldn't have believed that anyone in upper management would have expressed that opinion in such cold terms.

An atmosphere of policy changes and a number of consultant studies became the topics of conversations at regular luncheon gatherings in the Tower's cafeteria, in the Tower's lowest level. My close associates and I would discuss a range of issues like the icy winter, the Cubs or Bears, current Sears' events, and increasing use of consultants that led to major changes in company policy.

We would sarcastically refer to the manner in which the consultants would meet with knowledgeable Sears' staff to glean all they could concerning the subject of their study, and use the veterans' input to create power-point presentations that were designed to fit the predisposed positions of the company's officers and the Board.

Further changes was marked In May 1979, when Sears management learned that a consulting firm was contracted to evaluate compensation at every level by implementing a matrix that would measure decision making responsibility. The study's conclusion shifted substantial responsibility from middle management toward upper levels of management and rested the greatest degree of responsibility to the CEO. The result was that higher management levels were credited with greater job value and higher compensation, which may result in lower ranked employees receiving longer spans between pay increases that were smaller.

According to *Payscale.com*, in 1970 CEO salary and bonus packages were typically 25 times the average production worker that grew to 90 times the average production worker's salary by 2000, and I suspect the pay spread grew at Sears in a similar fashion, but most importantly the new pay scale reflected management's unfortunate downgrading the value attributed to the contributions made by their lower ranked employees.

My concerns for Catalog were heightened, when the 1979 National Division 200 engineered profit and loss (P&L) statement, was released by the national operating department that once again indicated that the retail stores' catalog (D/200) business was unprofitable. But it was only a year into the Catalog Order Entry system's national installation and I expected that many of the system's efficiencies shouldn't show their impact so soon.

Another challenge to the anticipated effectiveness of the Catalog Order Entry system arose, when it was reported that the number of catalog customers had experienced its first decline in 25 years. It required me to explain that a reduction in the customer index should be anticipated, because one feature of the COE system was the verification of customer's name and address that would help eliminate customer duplications. A reduction in duplications would result in a more accurate customer index and more effective media distribution.

At this time I remained concern that upper management questioned Catalog's profitability in view of the loss shown on the 1979 National Division 200 P&L and leadership's impatience to see results from their investment in the newly installed COE system. While profitability of Division 200 continued to be questioned, because its performance was buried in retail stores, the catalog stores' performance could be determined and in 1979 catalog stores reported a healthy growth that rose to 1,472 merchants and agents that developed net sales of $570 million.

The independent Merchants were stores that looked much like company owned catalog sales offices, and Agents were located in the smallest markets and conducted catalog business in addition to their non-Sears business.

In June 1980, Southern Territory Vice President, Ed Brennan arrived in Chicago to replace Dean Swift as President, and rumors of changes ran rampant on the Tower's floors, changes that would impact catalog and me directly. Near the end of the year, catalog's vice president, Jack Kelly, entered my office and broke the news that he was retiring at year's end. Kelly had overseen the catalog business from headquarters longer than anyone, save the founder, Richard Sears. When Kelly told me he was retiring, he impressed me as a man that had fought the good fight, but lost. Kelly retired December 30, 1980.

In the following year, the Catalog's Vice President's position was left unfilled that instantly created a void in Catalog's influence at a time that Wal-Mart had overtaken Sears as the nation's largest merchant.

In January 1981, I attended a meeting with Charlie Moran, the Eastern Territory's Operating Manager, who had arrived in headquarters as Vice President of Operating. Also in attendance was Al Stewart, who was a familiar figure from my days in the Eastern Territory, when he was an assistant to Moran. I recalled that Moran had confronted me to wonder if I really had brass balls, and Al Stewart had travelled with me in New England to evaluate my Division 200 payroll planner.

The meeting began with pleasantries and reminisces, but was followed by being advised that my position would change from National Catalog Selling Unit Manager to National Director of Catalog Operations within the operating department under the new National Operating Manager, Al Stewart. I was advised that my catalog operations staff would include assistants for each category of catalog units, Division 200, catalog sales offices, and catalog sales merchants and agents.

My new office was smaller and my position's stature was even smaller, but my greatest disappointment was the fact that I would not be a member of a newly created monthly catalog planning meeting. The meeting was attended by all the national merchandise managers, including Al Stewart, not I, a fact that I deeply resented.

Instead of having the ability to provide direct input at these important meetings, I was relegated to responding to the committee's issues and decisions passed down to me by Al Stewart. That should have been the handwriting on the wall for me. In the New Year, my change in assignment coincided with Ed Brennan's replacement of Ed Telling as Chairman and CEO of the Sears Merchandise Group as Telling assumed the position as the newly established corporation's chief executive officer.

CATALOG SHIPPING AND HANDLING CHARGES

Since Vice President Kelly had not been replaced, the company's catalog division continued to be run by the catalog planning committee. The definition of a committee's design of a horse couldn't be truer: "A committee was formed to design a horse, but created a camel."

An example of the committee's misdirection occurred when I was charged to create a major change to our shipping and handling rate structure. The policy had been that every order would include a charge that would cover the shipping and handling cost of each order, but in the desire to increase single item orders like one shirt, one blouse, and one tie, I was directed to lower minimum shipping and handling charges. This misguided premise was contrary to the long held conviction that minimum shipping and handling charges were needed to approximate each order's shipping and handling costs.

Previously, when a customer ordered a single item and objected to the shipping and handling charge in relationship to the item ordered, salespeople would encourage the customer to order additional items to defray the shipping and handling charges that would be only a small amount more.

Even though revenue from catalog's shipping and handling charges was a large and vital revenue source for the catalog business, my objections were ignored, and I was scheduled to present the lower minimum shipping and handling charges to a meeting of the entire catalog merchandising staff. My objection to pretending support and making the presentation must have affected me physically, because on the day of the presentation I awoke with a horrific sore throat and a severe hoarseness.

When I faced my audience of the company's merchants, instead of talking through my slide show, I croaked through the entire presentation. The audience appeared to be more interested in making a single item sale than concern for the sale's profitability. The merchants, especially soft-lines merchants, overlooked my pained voice and cheered loudly. In the ensuing years, shipping and handling charge revenue was impacted and no clear improvement in soft-line sales could be detected.

Today's Internet marketers evidently use shipping and handling charges as a major revenue source that may even exceed the value of the item being sold, which underlines how misdirected the Sears' merchants were in promoting the reduction in minimum shipping and handling charges. A while ago, it appears that the Sears' internet business has recognized the importance of shipping and handling revenue, when I ordered an $8.00 item and the shipping and handling charge was $8.03. Due to the direction of the catalog planning committee, the impact of encouraging single item orders that would impact shipping and handling revenue was just one more nail in Catalog's coffin.

By 1981, the internet and on-line shopping was still only a twinkle in a tech's eye, but Ron Ramseyer, who headed catalog's media department, initiated a prototype of the 236 page Summer Catalog on a new technology, the video disk. The disk Ramseyer developed dramatically presented a video demonstration and voice description of merchandise that was represented on the Summer Catalog's paper pages. Because the cost of the video disk's production and distribution were seen as major drawbacks, upper management nixed further exploration of Ramseyer's brain child.

Ron's concept for catalog merchandise presentation was ahead of its time, but was headed in a promising direction. The disk's voice and video presentation of the Summer Catalog's pages of merchandise was innovative and might have application in today's internet merchandising. Instead of only internet-marketing pages of still pictures of merchandise, certain categories of merchandise presented with videos and dialogue could be an effective marketing method within a catalog format on the internet.

CHAPTER TEN
CATALOG RESTRUCTURE

With Telling at the corporate helm of Sears in the 1980s a major transformation began to take shape with actions to consolidate headquarters' departments, and administrative territories, groups, and zones. Several catalog plants were closed and the remaining plants became cost centers rather than profit centers. As associates lost their jobs to reorganization a sense of career insecurity began to be felt in the Tower and field.

In 1981, while Sears moved to make its merchandising and distribution structure smaller and more efficient, employees had to be encouraged by Telling's progressive actions in his acquisitions of Caldwell Banker's real estate firm and Dean Witter Reynolds' brokerage house. Soon after, Telling announced the establishment of the company's Discover card.

The financial acquisitions were viewed favorably by the stock market, but to develop the systems to accommodate the financial acquisitions set aside refinements in the company's merchandising, distribution and operation systems, as well as stall my own effort to introduce improvements to catalog systems.

An article published in Crains in January 24, 1989 reflected my own feeling, when it stated, "The strategy (financial moves) boosted revenue, but it sucked attention and resources from Sears' traditional merchandising core." Similarly, Sears' financial strategy might have delayed its attention to the marketing potential of the internet revolution.

In 1982, Bill Bass was promoted from his Washington Group Manager's post and named Senior Executive Vice President Field. From my positions in the New York Group, Eastern Territory and headquarters, I had the opportunity to work with Bass as the New York Group B store manager, White Plains, NY store manager, and Washington Group manager. Bass went on to become President of the Merchandise Group. I had hoped that our joint experiences might have led to greater consideration for the catalog business, but I was destined to be disappointed.

During 1982 and 1983, new strategies emerged to reduce cost and improve retail store's efficiencies. The development of the first retail Store of the Future in Vernon Hills, IL was led by Mike Bozic, and supported by Claude Ireson in store design and Charles Reaves in operations. I remembered Bozic as an operating assistant from my meeting with Ed Brennan in the Western New York Group. Mike Bozic continued his climb in the company, when in 1984 he was appointed President and Chief Operating Officer of Sears Canada. In 1987, Bozic replaced Bill Bass as President of Sears Merchandise Group.

The Store of the Future focused on merchandise departments' layout and design and key operational advancements with Central Cashiers and a warehouse pickup system. Included in the Store of the Future Claude Ireson developed an attractive redesign of Division 200's catalog counter and Self Service pickup, and I demonstrated Ireson's design at the Vernon Hills, IL officers' review.

The focus on operating efficiencies and organization didn't end with Store of the Future. By 1983 management personnel had been reduced from 20,000 to 14,000, the Southwest Territory was closed, retail administrative groups were reduced from 51 to 46, and one-half of the retail distribution centers were closed, from 110 to 55.

During this cost cutting period, the emphasis to reduce catalog costs turned to diverting a portion of general catalogs' distribution from mailing catalogs to existing higher level customers and diverting a portion to be sold in the selling units. The catalog was to be sold for $5, accompanied by a discount on the customer's first purchase.

When the plan to sell catalogs was first proposed, I advanced my experience in New York where a supplementary amount of catalogs were offered free to customers with Sears Revolving Charge accounts. I touted the favorable results in retail and catalog sales, and cited studies that found retail customers pre-shopped the catalog and bought as much as 25% more than retail customers without catalogs. Another study found that 70% of all U.S. households with annual income above $36,000 held a Sears credit card, a good target group of customers to promote with a catalog, but my status was not large or loud enough to be heard outside the catalog planning committee's discussions and decisions.

SALE OF THE CATALOG

My New York proposal to offer a free catalog to revolving charge customers was ignored and the program to sell catalogs began. The sale of the catalog may have been superior to mailing catalogs to lower value customers. However, on too many of my selling unit visits, weeks and months after the general catalogs' (The Big Books) mailed distribution had begun, I was disappointed to discover catalogs sitting in stacks in stores, not in customers' hands, and not producing sales. I concluded that the sale of catalogs program was a poor economical choice, because it delayed distribution into the hands of the consumer, unsold catalogs in stacks in stores produced no sales, and it was a time that catalog sales were struggling.

SALES FLYERS

By 1985 every aspect of the catalog business was being scrutinized, and change for change's sake seemed to be the order of the day. A new National Catalog Merchandise Manager made a big splash by changing the release dates of sales flyers and their identifiers. For example, the October sales flyer was newly identified as OT, instead of LE, and the effective mailing date was changed to more closely correspond with an October release.

At a meeting of retail and catalog merchants, announcement of this change was met with roaring applause. Standing at the back of the meeting room, I shook my head and couldn't help but be amused by the crowd's roar of approval. I couldn't see how changes in media identifiers could improve sales by a single dollar. Catalog veterans knew that LE was the code for the so-called October flyer, but most importantly the release and effective date had been determined to avoid cyclical slumps in sales and not tied to the beginning of a month.

Other merchandising moves began to be employed. The Big Book was split into an annual 1,088 page Home catalog and two seasonal 348 page Style catalogs for Spring and Fall in an effort to improve merchandising results and reduce catalog printing and circulation costs. The Home catalog's merchandise focus was mostly on appliances, hardware, auto, and leisure. The Style catalog featured apparel.

An Edsel-like strategy was introduced in 1989 in retail and catalog that deemphasized sale prices by a conversion to "Every Day Low Prices." Where an item's price point might have been traditional merchandising price points like $3.99 or $3.77, the customer was supposed to believe that $3.83 was an Every Day Low Price, a rock bottom price. Retail and catalog customers, who had been attuned to sale prices, weren't convinced that the so-called Every Day Low Prices was a true bargain, and the program was dropped after a single merchandising cycle.

In 2012, it's interesting to note that a struggling J C Penney announced the same merchandising strategy with "Every Day Low Prices." Penney's management must not have done a lot of research, because they didn't recognize that 30 years earlier Sears' "Every Day Low Prices" experience was a failure. J C Penney's own "Every Day Low Prices" marketing strategy met the same fate that Sears had endured.

When Ed Telling retired, Ed Brennan replaced him in 1986 as corporate Chairman, and Bill Bass became Chairman and CEO of the Merchandise Group. Brennan appointed Charles Reaves as the National Operating Manager to replace Al Stewart. Reaves took on a major effort to direct the development of an in-house point of sale and distribution system. My attempt to include the second phase of the COE returns handling order entry system was blocked, even though I pressed as hard as I could for the system – maybe too hard.

If Telling's influence had anything to do with my position in headquarters, his retirement may have triggered my transfer from National Director of Catalog Operations to assistant positions in the National Merchandise and Transportation departments. With Brennan now in control of the corporation and Bass as CEO of the Merchandise Group, I had hoped my years of interaction with both men would have benefited me, but I was transferred from the catalog division and I was left to assume that the two officers chose to go with a change in direction.

Soon after my reassignment I was informed that the 1986 National 200 Engineered P&L recorded a profit for the first time after reporting a loss for many years. That was encouraging news for me, because it supported my conviction that initiation of the order entry system, self-service pickup, and the notification system efficiencies would improve sales and reduce costs and returns. At that time, I could only wish that I could have remained with Catalog, because I was convinced there was a lot more to be accomplished.

The remaining six years of Catalog's existence went through dramatic changes. During the following three years away from Catalog while in the national merchandising and transportation departments, I remained positive by broadening knowledge in my new assignments in the two departments, and I took it as an opportunity to develop a degree of expertise in the newly introduced Lotus spreadsheet system.

Knowledge of the Lotus system with spreadsheet macros allowed me to develop various operating matrices that monitored transportations costs, merchandise and catalog shipments, and individual merchandise divisions' profitability. Development of Lotus spread sheets and complex macros may have been better accomplished with sophisticated computer programming, but with an IBM desk PC and the Lotus system, I was able to create complex analyses and processes without the need for technical assistance.

In my work in the merchandise and transportation departments I developed an appreciation of my fellow associates' performance in efficiently servicing the selling units and distribution centers at the least possible cost. As an example, one of my responsibilities in the transportation department was to monitor the cost of catalog merchandise shipments to Alaska while others in the department did similar work that accomplished significant transportation savings. It's likely that a number of these same department experts were subject to the company's force reductions to reduce payroll costs, but their payroll savings may well have been less than their work produced in the reduction of transportation costs.

Meanwhile the catalog business declined in sales from its peak of $3.9 billion in 1984 to $3.5 billion in 1987, and catalog's percentage of company sales fell from a 1980s high of 20.4% to 15.5% in 1987.

Chairman Brennan must have recognized that something had to be done to stem catalog's slide in sales and restore its contribution to the corporation. In 1989 Brennan named Everett Buckhardt, the former Boston Group Manager, as Executive Vice President of Catalog and Direct Marketing, and Buckhardt quickly launched a new course for the company's catalog business.

Over an 18 month period Catalog Merchandise Distribution Centers (CMDC) were reduced from ten to six. Because of my sixteen years in the Philadelphia region and appreciation for years of association with the outstanding employees of the catalog plant, it was a particularly sad note for me when the *Philadelphia Inquirer* announced on January 24, 1989 that the impressive landmark tower building on Roosevelt Boulevard, the Philadelphia catalog plant, would close in 1990 and 3,400 employees' jobs would be lost.

In conjunction with the catalog plant closings, catalog inventory was detached from retail as Charles Reaves, now President and CEO of Sears Logistics, relocated retail merchandise distribution into a network of retail distribution centers. **Retail stores' inventory transfer to retail distribution centers eliminated the**

catalog plants' distribution revenue it had received from retail and impacted catalog plants' overhead costs.

With Vice President Buckhardt's leadership, Catalog became its own company within Sears and a separate profit center. Because Sears planned to move out of the Tower to Hoffman Estates, a western Chicago suburb, Buckhardt relocated his catalog organization to the former Allstate building in Skokie, IL until Hoffman Estates would be ready for occupation in the company's new headquarters.

When Buckhardt was the Boston Group Manager, he had made an independent move to create a telephone central in Boston's market area, but now the Vice President had bigger plans by directing the development of a sophisticated telephone central system to be installed into a national network of telephone centrals in strategic areas around the country. A toll-free 800 number was established for catalog orders where the telephone centrals practically eliminated all telephone and counter orders taken by 2,300 retail and catalog selling units.

The telephone centrals' Advanced Catalog Order Entry System was a superior selling tool and had management control features that happily included the very same customer returns handling system enhancement that I had fought for ten years to initiate.

About a year after Buckhardt had assumed the Vice President's position, I was invited to return to the catalog organization as Catalog Logistics Analyst in a new Department of Catalog Logistics headed by the National Director, Tom Graham. In my capacity as Logistics Analyst, I took the opportunity to make my first visit to a telephone central in Provo, UT. I was thoroughly impressed by the professionalism, atmosphere, and spirit of the central. Management encouraged hugging and pats on the back, which seemed to me to be a surprising but pleasant way of doing business.

The telephone central unit clearly benefited from the Advanced Catalog Order Entry System that was an operator's dream through effective scheduling that provided effective customer service and included the ability to monitor an individual's productivity and returns performance. As much as my career may have been opposed to telephone centralization, I had to be impressed by the excellence of the Provo central and on further visits to other centrals. Most of my opposition to centralization was overcome by the professionalism of the national telephone centrals and the efficiencies of their Advanced Catalog Oder Entry system.

SELLING UNITS DIVORCED FROM CATALOG

In addition to the telephone centrals receiving all catalog orders, an effort was initiated to reduce order pickup handling in the selling units and daily shipping costs of catalog merchandise to the selling units by encouraging direct delivery to the customer by mail or truck and a store pickup strategy that shipped to the stores mail-sized packages in cartons by UPS and non-mail-sized items by truck on a reduced number of days.

My years of experience indicated that the result of reduced service to the stores and customers, removal of order taking by the selling units, and diminished catalog customer pickup traffic in the catalog stores units was a strategy that could

negatively influence sales and returns. In an effort to offer a faster service to customers, I helped establish an optional FEDX service for the customer and promoted the FEDX service on the 1989 December issue of Catalog Age.

Not only a catalog issue, but other major changes in company policy were the announcements of Brand Central in 1990 and the acceptance of the Visa and Master cards in 1992. The strategy to introduce Brand Central was designed to expand appliance and electronics offerings to consumers by selling the Sears brands as well as other industry's brands in retail stores and catalogs. Like Brand Central, the acceptance of credit cards other than Sears and Discover credit cards was intended to expand the consumer base.

As a Sears veteran I believed Brand Central and the acceptance of other credit cards created a loss in Sears exclusivity. From the time I first joined Sears I felt the exclusiveness of Sears named products like Kenmore and Craftsman had a favorable result in merchandise gross profit and pricing and created more of an appeal to consumers rather than a detriment to sales, but that's just me.

When Arthur Martinez in 1992 arrived from Saks Fifth Avenue to take the helm as Chairman and CEO of the Merchandise Group, he introduced a marketing plan called "The Softer Side of Sears." The "Softer Side" strategy attempted to convert Sears' image from work clothes, fencing, Craftsman tools and Kenmore appliances to a focus on a major revamp of the larger retail stores that would make the Sears retail department stores look more like fashionable Nieman Marcus or Saks department stores.

It was interesting to read an article from *The Press* that reported in 1993, "His (Martinez) Brooklyn, NY family neither shopped at Sears nor ordered from the Sears catalog." Martinez's retail emphasis on "Softer Side of Sears" and never experiencing the ease and value in catalog shopping was a fact that didn't bode well for catalog's future.

CHAPTER ELEVEN

LEGACY LOST

As I have highlighted in the preceding chapters, over a span of thirty years a number of the merchandising changes and cost cutting efforts implemented were counterproductive: Eliminating the Early Shoppers Discount that had marketing, merchandising, and operating benefits, selling the catalog instead of considering a more effective distribution method, minimizing the value of promotional calling that had provable sales results, lowering shipping and handling charges on single item orders that negatively affected additional sales and shipping and handling revenue, eliminating next day delivery that negatively influenced customer service, sales, and returns, and reducing catalog plants' delivery days to the stores that impacted customer service, sales and returns and discouraged store pickup that affected store traffic and retail sales.

Following twenty years of interesting, enjoyable, and satisfying events, my final years experienced incidents of frustrations and lack of challenges. Most likely many catalog employees would have shared similar disappointments. Reorganizations, layoffs, fits and throes in corporate direction, cost cutting, and massive layoffs created scars in personal security that couldn't be readily overcome.

In the waning months of Catalog's existence and in my final visits in the field, I focused on stores and regions that experienced extremely high rates of customer returns. In my experience high return rates were symptomatic of a selling unit's operational deficiencies. Ineffective customer service, poor order follow-up, inadequate personnel, and lax management were some of the main causes of abnormally high customer returns.

In some visits to D/200 units with high returns, I discovered an uncommon condition of uninvolved management and a lack of spirit that was once the hallmark of a store's Division 200, which explained much of the reason for their failure to control customer returns. The large quantity of unsold catalogs stacked in the backrooms was another indication of ineffective management.

In a final catalog plant visit, my experience at the shipping dock was indicative of the decline in the catalog plants' professionalism and conscientiousness that I had admired during my entire career. When a staff member and I arrived at the shipping dock, I noticed a large number of camcorders stacked for shipment by FEDX. The large number of camcorders stoked my curiosity, and I asked the dock staff if this was an unusual day for so many camcorder shipments. I was told that they didn't believe so, but not accepting the vague response, the plant's staff member and I examined the shipping labels and discovered that the destination addresses were identical for all the camcorders.

Within an hour it was verified that the camcorders' destination was a vacant lot not far from the catalog plant. I left hoping further investigation would reveal what person(s) may have been involved in this obvious scam. In prior years this type of criminal activity would never have been overlooked by the catalog plant's personnel.

During my final years at Sears I served on a task force made up of several Sears executives and Arthur Andersen consultants. Ostensibly, our group's mission was formed to develop a plan that would direct catalog onto a more profitable course. Our task force met regularly in the National Logistics headquarters conference room.

My Lotus spreadsheet with its series of macros that incorporated data on gross profit and operating costs for each merchandise division's lines and items was the tool used to determine the effect of the task force members' recommended changes to the merchandise structure. We studied a number of scenarios that tailored product lines, reduced the number of catalog distribution centers, and made changes in catalog distribution that measured the impact on sales, costs, and profit. Each of the Lotus spreadsheet's scenarios produced a different result in sales and profit improvement.

My spreadsheets and our scenarios' results were left in the hands of the Anderson consultants that were tasked to produce a report and a recommendation to the corporate officers and eventually the Board. Even though I had been a working member of the task force, I was not privy to Anderson's final product.

As much as I wished for the best possible action from our study, I was cognizant of the bias toward Catalog and measures that were taken over years that curtailed catalog's growth, which caused me to harbor concerns that no good may be realized from our task force's options. I feared that it was preordained that Catalog would be dissolved, and we had gone through the motions to satisfy the corporate officers and board of directors' predispositions.

My fears were realized, when Arthur Anderson processed the work of the task force, and the consultants developed their proposal to the Board. I could only imagine that Andersen prepared a marvelous power-point show that may have told corporate management what they hoped to hear.

The Board's announcement entailed: The killing of the Big Book, closing the distribution centers, disbanding the catalog stores and the independent catalog selling units, a reliance on specialized catalogs and internet marketing to salvage some portion of catalog sales, and a hope that retail stores would be able to capture a major portion of lost catalog sales.

The Board's decision occurred despite Catalog Vice President Buckhardt's decisive moves that established Catalog as a separate company and a definitive profit division, dramatically reduced costs by trimming the organization and distribution centers, directed the development of a professional telephone centralization network with a state of the art Advanced Catalog Order Entry System, and development of a sophisticated direct marketing business. It became apparent that Buckhardt's efforts and accomplishments within a span of only three years were discounted by the officers' underlying considerations to end Catalog.

When Sears abandoned a catalog business that had risen to $4 billion in sales and built on a network of 13 catalog distribution centers, 2,500 selling units, and a distribution of 350 million catalogs to 25 million households, there lacked an aggressive plan to retain a lion share of its catalog business and the opportunity to develop new business. The aim that much of the catalog sales could be diverted more profitably to retail stores may have caused the company to minimize the opportunity to pursue the internet market. It's not coincidental that Amazon emerged in 1994, only one year after the Big Book and Catalog were jettisoned.

A 1999 article by Crain's David Snyder reported, "Sears had a chance to be an early internet leader. It was once a 50% owner of Prodigy – one of the first commercialized online services." Within just three years after closing Catalog, "Martinez sold Sears' Prodigy stake in 1996 for an estimated $125 million." Snyder went on to indicate Sears also had a 30% stake in Advantis and sold it to IBM for $450 million in 1997. Advantis was a high speed data networking company.

After reading the *Fortune* article in January 9, 2012 that headlined, "How Amazon Ate Sears Lunch" and the 1999 Crain article, I was stunned that Sears failed to take advantage of its leadership in catalog, technology, and distribution. Prior to the close of the catalog business in 1993, it appears that Catalog Vice President Buckhardt had positioned Sears to be a dominant e commerce player, but in just three years after closing Catalog, the company must have recalculated its internet direction and cashed in on its technology. The divestiture of Prodigy and Advantis is sufficient evidence that Sears surrendered the opportunity to challenge Amazon's leadership in internet marketing.

In order to determine the level of sales after 1993 that might be comparable to historical catalog sales totals, I referred to the Sears 1998 Annual Report, but I was unable to isolate the comparable sales data I sought, because internet sales was incorporated under a heading "Services" with a host of business items: Product repair, service contracts, home improvements, pest control, carpet cleaning, direct response marketing, markets insurance (credit, life, health), clubs and service membership, merchandise through specialty catalogs, merchandise for sale via company web sites. "Services" totaled $375 million in 1998. Catalog sales totaled $3.9 billion in 1984.

Nostalgia from my career in Catalog is not to suggest that the Big Book should have been saved, but it's regrettable that the "war" that existed between retail and catalog factions may have clouded the corporate view of the opportunity to recalibrate its marketing strategy and initiate a plan to seize internet marketing supremacy.

Even as consumers have largely shifted their buying habits from catalog pages to on-line shopping, it has become evident that internet marketing is impacting the sales performance in brick and mortar stores as well, which should highlight that a major expansion in Sears Direct Sales (internet marketing) has greater importance. A dominant Direct Sales business could have the same synergistic effect on retail sales as the Big Book that acted as shopping reference for Sears' customers.

Andrea Ovan's 2014 Harvard Business Review article, Andrea echoed my own belief, "If Sears history tells us anything, it's that great business ideas in the hands of great CEOS are very effective and also very hard to sustain – but not impossible to keep on repeating."

Sears might still return to its former merchandising prominence by initiating an innovative Direct Sales business that sets its sights to compete with Amazon and other internet marketers by initiating the electronic marketing of a catalog-sized range of merchandise, an action that could help energize another historic and optimistic course in Retail. With the accomplishment of this strategy, Sears could once again be the nation's premier merchant as directed more than 125 years ago by Sears' own greats, Richard Sears, Julius Rosenwald and General Robert E. Wood.

www.ingramcontent.com/pod-product-compliance
Lightning Source LLC
Chambersburg PA
CBHW050213230526
45470CB00001B/371